Just for Pat.

Contents

3

Dynamic Data Exchange—An Overview   29

8

OLE Servers   207

Introduction

Today, your Windows applications can't live in a vacuum. Users expect your program to share data with other applications such as Word and Excel. Although the clipboard is fine for some simple programs, more and more developers must support Dynamic Data Exchange (DDE) and Object Linking and Embedding (OLE).

OLE 2.0, the latest version, is a stepping stone between classic Windows and the new object-oriented operating systems expected soon. Applications that work with OLE 2.0 will likely have a significant head start when Microsoft releases these new operating systems.

Although DDE and OLE are important, they can also be difficult to implement because many topics are poorly documented. If you have plenty of time to spare, you can get started with OLE or DDE by finding some source code that works and studying it to learn its secrets. If you're lucky, the program you pick will work properly (otherwise you'll propagate its mistakes to your own code). However, if you don't have much time and you need to write programs fast, you need *OLE 2.0 and DDE Distilled*. You'll find the following topics covered:

- OLE 2.0 containers and servers
- Practical examples of OLE and DDE servers and clients
- A library that simplifies the creation of DDE servers
- Information about using C with OLE 2.0
- Comprehensive discussion of the clipboard, including ways to use the clipboard from DOS programs

OLE 2.0 and DDE Distilled emphasizes a quick return on your reading investment. Unlike most other Windows books, this one will help you start writing practical programs almost right away. Depending on your interests, there are several paths through the book, and you can select chapters according to your needs.

Special Features

The beginning of each chapter has a special header that describes the chapter's contents and what you need to know to get the most out of the chapter (see Chapter 1 for an example).

The disk included with this book contains the listings and WINBATCH, which is a shareware program from Wilson WindowWare. WINBATCH can interact with other programs using DDE, so it will work with the DDE examples in this book. It also has some support for OLE automation.

What You Will Need

The programs in this book will work with Borland C/C++ or Microsoft C/C++. You should also have the Windows SDK documentation either in book form or online. Unlike some other books that cover OLE, this one doesn't require that you use C++ or a special class library (like Microsoft's MFC). If you are still programming in C or use a non-Microsoft class library (like Borland's OWL, for example), you will have no problem working with the code in this book. However, if you use C++, you can still use the ideas and techniques in this book. There are even some methods you can use to simplify porting C code to C++ or using a mix of C and C++ in OLE programs.

The Road Map

Rather than read the chapters of this book in sequence, you might prefer skipping around. There are a few guidelines, however. Everyone should read Chapter 1 first. If you are an experienced Windows programmer and comfortable with the clipboard, you might skip Chapter 2; otherwise, read it after Chapter 1. Following that, you are on your own and can read just the chapters that interest you most. The following chart will help you find the chapters you want to read.

If you want to...	Go to...
Use the clipboard	Chapter 2
Communicate with DOS programs	Chapter 2
Understand DDE	Chapter 3
Write DDE clients	Chapter 4
Write DDE servers	Chapter 5
Write client-server applications	Chapter 3, 4, 5

1

Interprocess Communications

WHAT'S IN THIS CHAPTER

You'll learn about interprocess communications, which are the methods used to communicate between programs.

PREREQUISITES

None

1

When PC programming meant DOS programming, making programs communicate with each other was rarely a problem. Since DOS runs only one process at a time, true interprocess communication (IPC) was impossible. Although Terminate and Stay Resident programs (TSRs) try to multitask, and unrelated programs can communicate via files, two ordinary DOS programs cannot run simultaneously, much less communicate.

With the arrival of Windows, multitasking became a PC concern, and many questions resulted. For example, running multiple programs is easy, but how can these programs communicate? Can you transfer data from your database to a word-processing document? Get live stock quotes from a terminal program into a spreadsheet? These are some of the concerns that can be resolved by IPC.

Traditional multitasking systems such as UNIX have always supported rich IPC functions. Windows—especially Windows NT—also provides many IPC primitives. Some are similar to those found on UNIX and other systems, and others are more innovative.

Basic Forms of IPC

There are four primary means by which Windows programs can communicate with each other:

- Message passing
- The clipboard
- Dynamic Data Exchange (DDE)
- Object Linking and Embedding (OLE)

At first glance, message passing seems ideal for IPC. A simple SendMessage() or PostMessage() call can deliver a message (even a user-defined message) to any window. This message could even contain a shared global memory handle; see the GMEM_DDESHARE flag for GlobalAlloc().

Upon closer examination, this method has several problems. What window is the target of your message? What data can the other program return? Clearly, Windows needs a more comprehensive protocol to implement IPC.

The clipboard is probably the most common and simplest form of IPC. A program places data (usually in multiple formats) on the clipboard. Later, any program (including the same application) can search the clipboard. If it finds a format that it can use, it can read the contents of the clipboard. Nearly all clipboard operations result from user commands and complete (or fail) immediately.

Because DDE allows programs to request data from other applications, you can think of DDE as a dynamic clipboard. With the clipboard, you might copy sales information from a spreadsheet on the clipboard and paste it into a document. With DDE, the document can start the spreadsheet (if it isn't already running), load the proper worksheet, and read the contents of a specific cell.

In the previous example, the document is the DDE client, and the spreadsheet is the server (the traditional client-server architecture). Notice that the transaction is similar to an automated clipboard transaction in that the two programs still must agree on a format that both understand.

OLE bypasses this problem and allows you to paste sound, graphics, or any other OLE server data into other documents. The client reserves an area for the server's data; it neither manipulates nor understands the data—it only displays, prints, and stores it. The server then manages the display of the data.

Advanced OLE programs can gain access to data directly. Used in this way, OLE can replace the need for DDE. However, for programs that need multiple connections or high-speed data links, DDE is still a good choice.

Potential Problems with IPC

IPC has several problems not found in most other areas of programming. For example, if one program wants to read a graphic from the clipboard, it must use the same format as the program that put it there. When a word processor places text on the clipboard, should it be a graphic image of the text (so that fonts are visible), ASCII text, or a private format that encapsulates the font and style? Perhaps it should supply all three (or even more) formats.

Passing pointers via IPC is usually a bad idea. On systems like Windows NT, each process runs in its own address space. A valid pointer for one program is, at best, invalid for another program (at worst, it's valid, but points to something totally unrelated). Even under ordinary Windows, it is possible to have pointers that are not valid for each process.

As IPC crosses network boundaries, things become even more problematic. For example, passing pointers between machines is not possible; instead, the program must pass the entire data object. Then, the receiver synthesizes a new pointer with the copied data. Of course, you also need a mechanism for keeping the data on both ends of the transaction synchronized. An additional problem is that some machines use different ordering of bytes and character sets. Any IPC mechanism that works across networks must take these issues into account.

Summary

IPC is a collection of methods used to allow different processes to communicate. Some IPC methods, like the clipboard, will even allow a process to talk to itself.

As your program communicates with other programs, it must be aware of the problems inherent in IPC programming. Each IPC method has different approaches to these problems as you will see in later chapters.

Windows IPC has three major flavors: the clipboard, DDE, and OLE. The clipboard is best for user-directed data transfers. Programs often use DDE for automated data links. OLE allows programs to incorporate data with no prior knowledge of the data's format.

At this point, you may or may not wish to proceed with Chapter 2. Even if you're interested only in DDE or OLE, you should read Chapter 2 before proceeding, since DDE and OLE both borrow ideas from the clipboard. However, if you're an experienced Windows programmer and fully understand the clipboard, you might refer to the road map in the introduction and skip directly to the chapters that interest you.

2

The Clipboard

WHAT'S IN THIS CHAPTER

This chapter covers the most common IPC mechanism, the Windows clipboard. The clipboard and its formats form the foundation for more sophisticated forms of IPC.

PREREQUISITES

Basic Windows programming concepts.

Windows users generally know about the clipboard. Most applications can place data on the clipboard (usually via a Cut or Copy command). Later, an application (which may be the same or different from the first program) can read the data (often via a Paste command).

At first glance, this seems simple enough. But behind the scenes, it is more complex than it appears. For example, if a word processor cuts formatted text to the clipboard, how should the text paste into a graphics program? Straight text? A bitmap of the text? Even two text-based programs can have trouble. For example, does a text string use the ANSI or OEM character set?

Behind the Scenes

In reality, the clipboard usually holds not just one item but many representations of an item. When a program places data on the clipboard, it renders it in as many different formats as possible. This allows other programs to select the desired format.

A word processor often places text on the clipboard in several formats. First, it probably uses a private format that it can read back. This way, if the user cuts and pastes in the same application, all formatting remains intact. Next, it might place Rich Text Format (RTF) on the clipboard since many applications can read RTF. Then it probably supplies plain ASCII text for simple programs like Notepad.

Not all clipboard elements have to represent the same thing. For example, when you place a bitmap on the clipboard, it has a format of CF_BITMAP (see Table 2-1 for a complete list of predefined clipboard formats). However, there is also an element of type CF_PALETTE that contains the palette information for the bitmap.

Table 2-1. Clipboard Formats

Function	Description
CF_TEXT	Ordinary text
CF_OEMTEXT	Text in machine character set
CF_BITMAP	Bitmap
CF_METAFILEPICT	Windows metafile
CF_SYLK	Excel format
CF_DIF	Data interchange format
CF_TIFF	TIFF graphics
CF_DIB	Device-independent bitmap
CF_PALETTE	Palette for bitmap (see text)
CF_PENDATA	Pen input
CF_RIFF	Resource
CF_WAVE	Sound file
CF_OWNERDISPLAY	Custom format
CF_DSPTEXT	Private text format (see text)
CF_DSPBITMAP	Private bit map format (see text)
CF_DSPMETAFILEPICT	Private metafile format (see text)
CF_UNICODETEXT[*]	Unicode text
CF_ENHMETAFILE[*]	Enhanced metafile

[*]Windows NT only

Windows treats the CF_TEXT and CF_OEMTEXT formats in a special way. CF_TEXT data is for strings that use the ANSI character set, which is the Windows default. CF_OEMTEXT uses the DOS character set. However, Windows can translate between these two sets; that is, if you place CF_TEXT on the clipboard and then try to read CF_OEMTEXT out, Windows will perform the conversion for you. Windows does not auto-matically convert any other formats.

Besides the types that appear in Table 2-1, an application can define private types. The program can use these types to transfer data to itself or to other cooperating applications. You'll see more about private formats later in this chapter.

Clipboard Access

The clipboard is a global resource that all Windows applica-tions share. Only one program owns and can have the clip-board at any given time. This program is the last one that calls EmptyClipboard()—not necessarily the last one to open the clipboard.

To claim the clipboard, you pass OpenClipboard() your window handle. The function returns zero if the clipboard is already open. You can then either show an error message to the user or wait and try again.

Table 2-2 shows the most useful clipboard functions. Call EmptyClipboard() to prepare the clipboard for new data, then call SetClipboardData() once for each format you want to write to the clipboard.

To read from the clipboard, you usually call IsClipboard-FormatAvailable() until you find a format you understand. Next, you open the clipboard and call GetClipboardData() to retrieve the data.

Instead of searching for an appropriate format, you can pass a list of formats to GetPriorityClipboardFormat(). This function examines an array that contains format codes (in order of preference) and returns the most preferred format that is currently available.

Table 2-2. The Windows Clipboard API

Function	Description
OpenClipboard()	Opens the clipboard
EmptyClipboard()	Removes current clipboard contents
SetClipboardData()	Places data on clipboard
IsClipboardFormatAvailable()	Queries clipboard for format
EnumClipboardFormats()	Lists available clipboard formats
GetClipboardFormatName()	Gets name of custom format
GetPriorityClipboardFormat()	Gets data in "best" format
GetClipboardData()	Reads data
CloseClipboard()	Closes the clipboard.
RegisterClipboardFormat()	Creates custom format
GetClipboardOwner()	Finds program that put data on clipboard last

Most formats use a global memory handle as the clipboard item. Once you write a handle to the clipboard using SetClipboardData(), you must not free it (also, it must not be locked). Once you pass a handle to SetClipboardData(), the clipboard owns it and will free it for you when necessary; this also applies to GetClipboardData(). If you want to modify the data, you should copy it to private storage at once.

When you have the data, you should call CloseClipboard(). Until you do, no other program can use the clipboard. It is bad form to hold the clipboard open between messages—worse still to open the clipboard and crash.

These basic steps apply to all clipboard transfers. You can find a summary of these procedures in the box entitled "The Clipboard: Step by Step."

The Clipboard Step-by-Step

Follow these simple steps to paste data from the clipboard or to cut or copy data to the clipboard.

Paste:

1.   Call IsClipboardFormatAvailable() or GetPriority-ClipboardFormat(). If no formats exist that you can use, report an error.

2.   Call OpenClipboard(). If unsuccessful, try again or report an error.

3.   Call GetClipboardData() to retrieve a global handle to the clipboard data.

4.   Copy data to private storage.

5.   Call CloseClipboard().

Cut/Copy:

1.   Copy data to global memory block. Once you give this block to the clipboard, you will not be able to access it.

2.   Repeat step 1 for each format your application can render.

3.   Release all locks on the memory block.

4.   Call OpenClipboard(). If unsuccessful, try again or report an error.

5.   Call EmptyClipboard().

6.   Call SetClipboardData() for each data format you can supply.

7.   Call CloseClipboard().

Special Formats

Although the predefined formats (see Table 2-1) cover most cases, sometimes you need a custom format or want to handle a predefined format in a special way. Windows allows you to create new clipboard formats and share them with other applications. There are also ways to have private formats and a method used to conserve memory when dealing with large clipboard items.

Delayed Formats

Imagine you are writing a general-purpose graphics editor. When the user copies an image to the clipboard, you want to supply the picture in bitmap, metafile, TIFF, and PCX format. However, rendering each of these formats could take some time (not to mention memory). If the user needs only the bitmap, the time and memory spent on the other formats are wasted.

To combat this problem, you can pass a NULL handle to SetClipboardData(). If the format is needed, Windows asks you to render it. You must handle the following three additional messages in your window function to achieve this:

1. WM_RENDERFORMAT—Place format specified by wParam on the clipboard, which will already be open.

2. WM_RENDERALLFORMATS—Open the clipboard and render all outstanding formats, and then close the clipboard. Windows sends this message as your application exits. You may ask the user if you should discard the clipboard contents instead of generating the data (Microsoft Publisher, for example, does this).

3. WM_DESTROYCLIPBOARD—This message means
    that you are no longer the clipboard owner. Therefore,
    you can discard any information you are saving solely
    to satisfy the first two messages.

You can mix delayed formats with ordinary formats. For
example, you can put a metafile in the clipboard and convert
it to bitmap format only if asked. Your program can even read
the metafile back from the clipboard to do the conversion.

Custom Formats

Besides the formats in Table 2-1, an application can create new
formats by calling RegisterClipboardFormat(). This function
takes a string that identifies the format and returns an
identifier that you can use with the clipboard functions. If
multiple applications call RegisterClipboardFormat() with the
same string, Windows returns the same format identifier. This
makes it possible for cooperating applications to share a clipboard format.

Of course, the clipboard viewer can't display a custom format,
but this is rarely a problem. For example, if a word processor
places formatted text on the clipboard, it usually puts plain
text (CF_TEXT) there as well. Then the clipboard viewer will
show the plain text (Windows even allows you to write your
own clipboard viewer if you are a masochist).

If your users insist on seeing formatted displays in the
clipboard viewer, you must take a different approach. Instead
of using RegisterClipboardFormat(), you can place custom
data on the clipboard with the CF_OWNERDISPLAY format.
Then you must process the same messages that delayed
formats require (see the earlier discussion) plus five more (see
Table 2-3). These messages allow you to update the clipboard

viewer's client area to represent your data. Unless you are concerned with users viewing your data with the clipboard viewer, this is probably more trouble than it's worth.

Table 2-3. CF_OWNERDRAW Messages

Message	Description	wParam	lParam
WM_RENDERFORMAT[*]	Provides specified format	format	N/A
WM_RENDERALLFORMATS[*]	Provides all outstanding formats	N/A	N/A
WM_DESTROYCLIPBOARD[*]	Discards clipboard information	N/A	N/A
WM_ASKCBFORMATNAME	Returns name of custom format	buf. len.	buffer
WM_SIZECLIPBOARD	Clipboard is changing size	viewer HWND	new RECT
WM_PAINTCLIPBOARD	Updates viewer window	viewer HWND	PAINTSTRUCT
WM_HSCROLLCLIPBOARD	Horizontal scroll viewer	viewer HWND	info
WM_VSCROLLCLIPBOARD	Vertical scroll viewer	viewer HWND	info

[*]Also used for delayed formats.

Display Formats

Another way to create semi-private formats is via the pre-defined display types (CF_DSPTEXT, CF_DSPBITMAP, and CF_DSPMETAFILEPICT). The clipboard viewer can display these formats, but they are hidden from ordinary applications. For example, if you place CF_DSPTEXT on the clipboard, an application looking for CF_TEXT won't find anything on the clipboard. A cooperating application that uses CF_DSPTEXT can retrieve your data, however.

Of course, there is no guarantee the data doesn't belong to another application using the CF_DSPTEXT format. To guard against this, you can use GetClipboardOwner() to find the clipboard owner's window handle and use GetClassName() to convert it to a class. You can then decide if it is a cooperating application. For text, you can add a unique prefix to the true data to distinguish it.

Clipping DOS

In 386 enhanced mode, DOS programs (running in a DOS box) can cut and paste items to the clipboard using interrupt 0x2F. Table 2-4 shows the API. Note that DOS programs can use only certain clipboard formats; in practice, anything other than text is too much trouble anyway.

Table 2-4. The DOS Box Clipboard API (INT 2FH)

Get WINOLDAP version

Input: AX=0x1700

Output: if AX=0x1700 then WINOLDAP does not support clipboard access
otherwise AL=major version, AH=minor version

Open Clipboard

Input: AX=0x1701

Output: AX=0 on failure

Clear Clipboard

Input: AX=0x1702

Output: AX=0 on failure

Table 2-4. The DOS Box Clipboard API (INT 2FH) (cont.)

Copy to Clipboard

Input: AX=0x1703

DX=format code (see Table 2-1)

SI:CX=data length

ES:BX=pointer to data

Output: AX=0 on failure

Query Clipboard

Input: AX=0x1704

DX=format code (see Table 2-1)

Output: DX:AX=size of data (or zero if unavailable)

Paste from Clipboard

Input: AX=0x1705

DX=format code (see Table 2-1)

ES:BX=pointer to buffer

Output: AX=0 on failure

Close Clipboard

Input: AX=0x1708

Output: AX=0 on failure

Compact Clipboard

Input: AX=0x1709

SI:CX=required size

Output: DX:AX=Largest block available (or zero on error)

Putting data on the clipboard from DOS is simple. Just follow these steps:

1. Make sure Windows is running in 386 enhanced mode.

2. Make sure clipboard access is supported (function 0x1700).

3. Open the clipboard (function 0x1701).

4. Compact the clipboard (function 0x1709); make sure there is enough space for your data.

5. Copy your data using function 0x1703.

6. Close the clipboard (function 0x1708).

Reading the clipboard is nearly the reverse of the above:

1. Make sure Windows is running in 386 enhanced mode.

2. Make sure clipboard access is supported.

3. Open the clipboard.

4. Make sure the clipboard has the data type you need (function 0x1704).

5. Paste the data using function 0x1705.

6. Close the clipboard.

You'll see an example of these steps later in this chapter.

If you need to pass data between a DOS program and a Windows application, the clipboard is one way to do it. The bibliography contains an entry for a system that allows DOS programs to call nearly any Windows API call using this technique (see "Accessing the Windows API from the DOS Box," by Andrew Schulman, in the bibliography). You can also

use shared memory buffers allocated before Windows starts or inside a virtual device driver (VxD) as Microsoft's WX server does (see the bibliography entry for *DOS and Windows Protected Mode* for more about shared memory buffers).

A Simple Windows Example

WCLIPB.C is a simple Windows program written with the WPRINT library (see the box entitled "The WPRINT Library"). The program displays any text that is currently on the clipboard and allows you to place a new string in the clipboard. Listings 2-1 and 2-2 show pertinent excerpts from WCLIPB.C (the entire listing and its supporting files are on the companion disk; also, see the box entitled "About the Listings").

The WPRINT Library

The WPRINT library first appeared in *Commando Windows Programming* (see the bibliography). It provides two functions, win_input() and win_printf(), that use dialogs and message boxes to provide simple input and printf-style output.

The win_printf() call's first argument becomes the window's title. The remaining arguments are the same as printf()'s. The win_input() function takes the same arguments and uses them to form a prompt string. It returns a pointer to a static string that contains the user's input. If there was no input, the first byte of the string will be zero.

To use WPRINT, you need to include WPRINT.H, link with WPRINT.OBJ, and include WPRINT.RC in your resource file.

About the Listings

Since this book contains many large listings, only pertinent excerpts appear in the text. The entire version of each listing appears on the companion disk. Each chapter has its own subdirectory (for example, CHAP02 for Chapter 2). Some chapters may have further subdirectories to delineate various projects within the chapter.

Listing 2-1. Reading the Clipboard (excerpt from WCLIPB.C)

```
/* Check for text on clipboard */
  if (IsClipboardFormatAvailable(CF_TEXT))
    {
    if (!OpenClipboard(NULL))
        {
no_open:
        win_printf("Clipboard Utility",
                   "Can't open clipboard");
        return FALSE;
        }
/* Get data */
    h=GetClipboardData(CF_TEXT);
    clpdat=GlobalLock(h);
/* copy data from global block to local storage */
    while (*p++=*clpdat++);
    GlobalUnlock(h);
    CloseClipboard();
    }
  else
    strcpy(clptxt,"<NONE>");
/* Show text */
  win_printf("Clipboard Utility","%s",clptxt);
```

Listing 2-2. Writing to the Clipboard (excerpt from WCLIPB.C)

```
/* Read input */
  input = win_input("Clipboard Utility",
        "New clipboard contents (ENTER to quit):");
  /* If user just hit enter, quit! */
  if (!*input)
    return FALSE;
/* Make global block to accomodate text */
  h=GlobalAlloc(GHND,strlen(input)+1);
  clpdat=GlobalLock(h);
/* move text */
  while (*clpdat++=*input++);
  GlobalUnlock(h);
  if (!OpenClipboard(NULL)) goto no_open;
  EmptyClipboard();
/* Transfer global handle to clipboard */
  SetClipboardData(CF_TEXT,h);
  CloseClipboard();
  return FALSE;
  }
```

The only unusual feature of WCLIPB is that it has no window (thanks to the WPRINT library). Therefore, it passes NULL to OpenClipboard(), which is unusual, but harmless. Any program calling GetClipboardOwner() receives a NULL.

A Windows/DOS Example

Using the clipboard from DOS is remarkably similar to using it from Windows; only the method of calling the API differs. Since the clipboard is one of the few Windows services you can access directly from a DOS program, you may need to use it to provide "live" communications between the DOS and

Windows worlds. For example, suppose you want to run a
DOS program from inside Windows, collect the output, and
process it in a Windows application. You can use files, but
then you need a way to synchronize the two programs (you
can't read the file in the Windows program until you finish
writing to it from DOS). Also, you can't easily communicate in
both directions at once.

A Better Way

A better answer is to collect the output in real time and pass it
using the Windows clipboard. That is exactly what CLIPSH.C
does (see Listing 2-3). CLIPSH hooks interrupt 0x29 (the DOS
CON driver interrupt) with its int29() function. When this
routine collects an entire line of output in the line array, the
flush_clip() function passes it to the clipboard.

Listing 2-3. CLIPSH's Interrupt 0x29 Handler

```
/* Add output character to buffer, if newline or full
   buffer, call flush_clip() */
void _far _interrupt int29(INTREGS)
  {
  if ((line[lp++]=(Rax&0xFF))=='\n'||lp>=sizeof(line))
    flush_clip();
  }
```

Before CLIPSH sends an output line to the clipboard, it waits
until the clipboard contains the string CLIPSH:RDY. Then it
places the line on the clipboard preceded by a hex FF byte. This
helps distinguish CLIPSH text from ordinary text (remember,
the DOS clipboard interface doesn't support custom formats).
If CLIPSH finds CLIPSH:ABT instead of CLIPSH:RDY, it
terminates the executing program.

When CLIPSH is finished, it places CLIPSH:END on the clip-board. This is the signal to any cooperating program that the output is complete. After CLIPSH installs the int29() function, it collects its command line arguments and passes them to the standard system() call. The int29() function then collects output from the child process—not CLIPSH itself.

If you can run a program and collect its output using the DOS redirection operator, it will work with CLIPSH. Of course, CLIPSH is for running programs that you ordinarily can't modify, such as DIR, CHKDSK, and PKUNZIP. If you are using your own programs, you can just output to the clip-board directly and bypass the interrupt 0x29 handling.

The Details

The heart of CLIPSH is the flush_clip() function (see Listing 2-4). Its first duty is to switch to a private stack (the int_stack array). This requires some simple assembly code and prevents CLIPSH from overrunning the interrupted program's stack, which may be quite small.

Next, CLIPSH enables interrupts. When an interrupt occurs (such as the interrupt 0x29 that triggered the flush_clip() function), the CPU automatically disables further interrupts until the service routine completes. However, flush_clip() may have to wait for a cooperating Windows program to place the CLIPSH:RDY command on the clipboard. While interrupts are disabled, no other programs can run. This causes a deadlock where CLIPSH is waiting for output from a program that can't execute. With interrupts enabled, other programs are free to run while CLIPSH is waiting. When CLIPSH is waiting, it uses interrupt 0x2F, function 0x1680, to release its time slice to Windows. This allows other programs to execute without waiting for CLIPSH's time slice to expire.

Listing 2-4. The flush_clip() Function

```
/* Flush line from buffer to clipboard */
void flush_clip()
   {
   static int oldss,oldsp;
   char *stacktop=int_stack+sizeof(int_stack);
/* Switch stacks */
   _asm {
     mov oldss,ss
     mov oldsp,sp
     mov dx,stacktop
     mov ax,ds
     mov ss,ax
     mov sp,dx
     }
/* Allow future interrupts */
   _enable();
   if (!clip_wait())
     {
/* Prefix string with hex FF */
     line[0]='\xFF';
/* Terminate string with NULL byte */
     line[lp]='\0';
/* Put line on clipboard */
     while (!clip_open()) win_yield();
     clip_copy(CLIP_TEXT,strlen(line)-2,line);
     clip_close();
     }
/* reset line pointer */
   lp=1;
/* switch stack back */
   _asm {
```

```
    mov ax,oldss

    mov dx,oldsp

    mov ss,ax

    mov sp,dx

    }

}
```

You may need a PIF file for CLIPSH unless your
_DEFAULT.PIF file happens to contain the proper settings.
You'll need the background processing box checked, and you
may want to give CLIPSH a high background priority.

An Example

The WZIP program (see Figure 2-1) uses CLIPSH to execute
PKUNZIP, a popular archive program from PKWARE. By
using file open dialogs, WZIP provides a simple interface to
PKUNZIP. Of course, PKUNZIP and CLIPSH must be in the
current directory or on your path.

Figure 2-1. WZIP

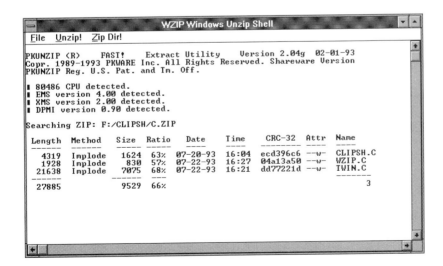

As you run WZIP, you will find that if the CLIPSH window is in the foreground, everything proceeds smoothly. However, if the CLIPSH window is in the background (or hidden) WZIP runs very slowly. Although it is more aesthetically pleasing to hide the CLIPSH program, the WZIP program usually runs too slowly to be useful.

Listing 2-5 shows the key to the WZIP program, the ClipExec() function. ClipExec() places the CLIPSH:RDY string on the clipboard and executes CLIPSH via WinExec(). As lines appear on the clipboard, WZIP uses the wputs() function to add lines to the edit control that serves as the main window (see EWINDOW.C).

Listing 2-5. The ClipExec() Function

```
ClipExec(HWND w,char *cmd)
   {
   int i;
   char *inline;
   PutClip(w,"CLIPSH:RDY");
/* Use SW_HIDE instead of SW_SHOW to make DOS window
   invisible (and very slow....) */
   if (WinExec(cmd,SW_SHOW)<32)
     {
     MessageBox(topwindow,"Can't execute command",NULL,
             MB_OK|MB_ICONSTOP);
     return 1;
     }
   inExec=1;
   for (i=0;i<100;i++) yield();
/* Uncomment the next line to make DOS window go background
   (slow...slow...slow) */
/*   SetWindowPos(w,NULL,0,0,0,0,SWP_NOSIZE|SWP_NOMOVE); */
   while (inline=ClipRead(w))
```

```
     {
     strcat(inline,"\r\n");
     wputs(inline);
     PutClip(w,"CLIPSH:RDY");
     }
   inExec=0;
   return 0;
   }
```

The Bad News

Of course, there is no free lunch. CLIPSH has some draw-backs. First, it destroys whatever is on the clipboard, which could annoy the unsuspecting user (see "Save Multiple Items to the Clipboard with CLIPSTAC" in the bibliography for some ideas on saving the clipboard contents). Also, any programs that output via the BIOS or require user interaction won't work properly.

Still, many useful DOS programs work with CLIPSH. By joining a Windows front-end to a DOS workhorse, you can write some surprisingly powerful programs quite easily. More important, as this example illustrates, the Windows clipboard is accessible from DOS programs. Your DOS programs can easily share data with Windows applications.

Summary

The clipboard is the most basic form of interprocess communications that Windows provides. You can use it to communicate with your application, other instances of your application, or other Windows programs. You can even communicate with DOS applications.

In the chapters on OLE, you will see an improved method of using the clipboard—OLE data objects. These objects allow you to transfer a small amount of data onto the clipboard and then retrieve specific data using OLE calls. This works even if the data source is not an OLE program. With data objects, you can request very specific renderings of data (for example, you might ask a picture for a 300 DPI monochrome bitmap copy of itself). Using data objects also simplifies OLE drag-and-drop operations. You'll learn more about OLE data objects in Chapters 6 and 7.

Although the clipboard is simple, it is the fundamental Windows IPC method. DDE transactions depend on sharing a clipboard data type (although DDE does not actually use the clipboard), and OLE transfers often (but not always) take the form of cutting and pasting links and objects to and from the clipboard.

3

Dynamic Data Exchange—An Overview

WHAT'S IN THIS CHAPTER

Dynamic Data Exchange is a protocol that allows programs to exchange data of known types and provides the basic foundation for implementing client-server applications. This chapter explains basic DDE terminology; Chapters 4 and 5 cover specifics about DDE.

PREREQUISITES

Understanding of Windows programming and clipboard formats.

Dynamic Data Exchange (DDE) is the basic foundation for client-server IPC under Windows. DDE corrects many limitations of the clipboard, for example, the destruction of existing data that occurs when an application places data on the clipboard. DDE can support multiple conversations, which are connections between two applications. Like the clipboard, both applications must agree on a data format.

Before delving into writing DDE applications, you should understand how DDE works from the user's perspective. You should also know some common DDE terminology.

When to Use DDE

DDE is suitable whenever you need to read data from another application for use in your own program. Here are some typical examples:

- Reading real-time temperature data from an instrument into a spreadsheet

- Transferring a result from a database into a word processor

- Passing a bitmap from one program to an image-processing program

Notice that DDE is best suited for data transfers that you wish to manipulate. For example, an image processor must manipulate the bitmap—not simply display it. If you want to place a bitmap in a word-processor document, using OLE is a better choice because the OLE server takes care of displaying and printing the bitmap. However, if you use OLE, you can't easily manipulate the data; it's the proverbial black box. Advanced OLE programs can peek inside the box and directly obtain an object's data. However, for real-time data transfers, DDE is usually much more efficient than the current implementation of OLE.

DDE servers can also accept commands from a client. For example, the Windows 3.1 Program Manager supports a set of commands that installation programs use to add groups and icons to it.

DDE and DDEML

When Microsoft introduced DDE, it was, to put it mildly, developer-hostile (as opposed to user-friendly). The protocol was difficult to understand and implement, which led to many incompatible interpretations of the standard as well as great frustration among users.

To help correct this problem, Microsoft now provides the DDE management library (DDEML), which is an API that greatly simplifies writing DDE applications. Although DDEML is new, programs written with it are compatible with applications that were written correctly without DDEML.

Because you should have no reason to write DDE programs without DDEML, this book covers only that method. Even if you have to maintain old-style code, you will have little difficulty if you understand DDEML.

Definitions

Like most areas of programming, DDE has its own jargon. An important part of learning DDE is getting a grasp on the terminology. Once you understand the following words and phrases, you will be well on your way to being a DDE programmer.

Client and Server

A **client** is a program that initiates a DDE conversation. Generally, but not always, a client requests data from a **server**, which usually supplies data. A program may be both client and server because it supplies data to some applications and reads data from others. Clients and servers both use a DDE callback function. This function is similar to an ordinary window function, except that Windows sends the DDE callback DDE-specific messages and parameters.

Conversation and Transaction

When a client connects to a server, it establishes a **conversation**. A message exchanged between a client and server constitutes a **transaction**.

A server can engage in conversations with multiple clients. Likewise, a client may hold conversations with many servers. You can distinguish between multiple conversations by examining the hConv parameter to the DDE callback.

Services, Topics, and Items

A DDE server is simply a Windows application that provides a **service**. The server has a service name that may or may not be unique to that application. For example, the Windows Program Manager (WPM) uses the service name PROGMAN. However, Norton Desktop for Windows (NDW) also uses PROGMAN because it provides the same services. A program that wants to use the service doesn't care if WPM or NDW provides it. However, for most applications it works best if the service name is the same as the program name. That way, if the server is not running, a potential client can start it by using that name.

Each server provides **topics**. For example, Word for Windows provides a topic for each open document. Servers usually support a system topic that provides common data that clients may need. Topics usually correspond to a document, but that is strictly up to the server. For example, a database might supply a topic for each record. The topic name would correspond to the record's primary key.

Each topic can contain many **items**. For example, the system topic usually provides an item that returns a list of available topics (the SZDDESYS_ITEM_TOPICS item). In Word for Windows, each bookmark is accessible as a DDE item. Our hypothetical database server's items would be database fields.

Services, topics, and items combine to create a three-level hierarchy (see Figure 3-1), which is similar to the file system. To open a file, you must know the drive it is on, its directory, and its file name. To obtain the value of an item, you must know the service name, the topic name, and the item name. For example, to access data from Word, you need to know Word's service name (WinWord), a topic (document) name, and the item name (a bookmark in that document).

The item's value can be any clipboard format. The client is responsible for interpreting or rendering the data just as it is with the clipboard. When a client obtains data from a server, it forms a **link** with the server.

Figure 3-1. DDE Hierarchy

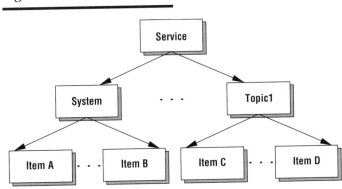

Cold Link

A client makes a **cold link** when it requests data from a server one time only. If the server's data changes, the client will not be aware of it.

Hot Link

A **hot link**, on the other hand, causes the server to retransmit the data to the client when it changes. This is useful for applications that need a continual data stream from another program.

Warm Link

A **warm link** is similar to a hot link with one exception: the server notifies the client when data has changed. It is up to the client to request the data again if it wants to update it.

DDE Commands

DDE servers can support a special form of transaction (the XTYP_EXECUTE transaction) that clients can use to execute commands on the server. This allows the client to ask the server to open a file, for example. Program Manager provides many commands to create groups and program items. Many installation programs use this capability to create groups automatically for their programs.

Handles

DDE applications must share strings and other data. DDE facilitates this with handles that can represent strings or data blocks. You create data handles with DdeCreateDataHandle() and strings with DdeCreateStringHandle() (Table 3-1 shows the handle-related calls.). You can use DdeCmpString-Handles() to compare string handles without case sensitivity.

Table 3-1. DDE Handle Functions

Function	Description
DdeAccessData()	Returns a pointer and length to data in a handle
DdeUnaccessData()	Releases a DdeAccessData() pointer
DdeAddData()	Adds data to an existing handle
DdeCreateDataHandle()	Makes a new data handle
DdeCreateStringHandle()	Makes a new string handle
DdeFreeDataHandle()	Releases a data handle
DdeFreeStringHandle()	Releases a string handle
DdeGetData()	Copies data from data handle to private buffer
DdeKeepStringHandle()	Increases string handle's reference count

Data transferred between server and client resides in HDDEDATA type handles. Strings that you send to DDEML to specify server, topic, and item names use HSZ string handles.

When you use DdeCreateDataHandle() to create a data handle, you can specify a data buffer for its initial contents. You can also add data to it later using DdeAddData(). The data handle also contains a string handle that identifies its item name. If the data handle does not correspond to an item (for example, when the item is an execute command), the item name must be NULL.

To learn the value of a string handle, use DdeQueryString-Handle(), which copies the string to a buffer of your choice. To work with a data handle's contents, you can use DdeAccessData(), which returns a far pointer to the data. When you are done, you must call DdeUnaccessData(). If you want to make a copy of the data, you may use DdeGetData().

The System Topic

Each DDE server can support multiple topics and items. To avoid confusion, most (but not all) servers support a SYSTEM topic that provides items that assist clients in accessing the server. Table 3-2 shows the typical items that a DDE server may support. For example, a client can ask for the TOPICS item under the SYSTEM topic to receive a list of topics that the server supports. When programming, it is best to use the defined constants instead of the actual string to ensure portability.

System topics that return lists (for example, SYSITEMS) return strings separated by tabs. When you build these strings, remember not to have tabs at the beginning or end of the list and to use only one tab per item. However, when reading these strings from other applications, don't assume how the string is formatted. Plan to strip leading tabs, multiple tabs, and tabs at the end of the string.

Table 3-2. Typical DDE Items

Topic	Constant	Description
SYSITEMS	SZDDESYS_ITEM_SYSITEMS	List of system topic items
TOPICS	SZDDESYS_ITEM_TOPICS	List of currently available topics
TOPICITEMLIST	SZDDE_ITEM_ITEMLIST	Items supported under non-system topics
FORMATS	SZDDESYS_ITEM_FORMATS	List of supported formats[*]
STATUS	SZDDESYS_ITEM_STATUS	Contains the string "READY" or "BUSY"
HELP	SZDDESYS_ITEM_HELP	General help information

[*]Often supported in system and non-system topics.

Summary

While DDE is somewhat complex, it is little more than a dynamic implementation of the clipboard. Of course, DDE doesn't actually use the clipboard, but it serves the same purpose. Whenever you need to pass data between applications programatically, you should consider DDE. However, if you simply want to render the data (that is, display and print it), use OLE instead and the OLE server will render the data for you.

4

Writing DDE Clients

WHAT'S IN THIS CHAPTER

This chapter shows how to write DDE clients. A DDE client can read and use data from DDE servers.

PREREQUISITES

Understanding of Windows programming, clipboard formats, and DDE concepts.

An application that requests data from other programs is a DDE client. With DDEML, writing DDE clients is a simple proposition. The simplest clients read data synchronously—that is, they issue a request and then wait for the server to respond. However, it is only slightly more complex to create asynchronous clients that receive data on the fly.

Client Structure

The basic flow of a typical DDE client is very simple. The client must

1. Initialize the DDEML library (DdeInitialize())

2. Connect to the server (DdeConnect() or DdeConnectList())

3. Perform data transactions (DdeClientTransaction())

4. Close the connection (DdeDisconnect() or DdeDisconnectList())

5. Terminate the DDEML library (DdeUninitialize()).

As you can see, all these operations map directly to DDEML calls.

Initialization

All clients must call DdeInitialize() to set up the DDEML library routines. Here is the prototype for DdeInitialize():

```
UINT DdeInitialize(DWORD FAR *dde_inst,PFNCALLBACK
callbk,DWORD cmd, DWORD reserved);
```

The first parameter is a pointer to a DWORD that receives the DDE instance handle for this client. Like the program's ordinary instance handle, this uniquely identifies the client to the DDEML library. Every DDE call requires this handle. When you first call DdeInitialize(), the variable that this parameter points to should contain zero. Otherwise, DDEML assumes you wish to reinitialize your DDE session using the specified handle. If the variable contains a random non-zero value, DDEML might get confused.

The callbk parameter is the function address for the client's DDE callback function. Like other callback functions, you'll get the address from MakeProcInstance() (unless you use the smart callbacks that some compilers offer—then it doesn't matter if you use MakeProcInstance() or not). Many simple clients don't require a callback, as you'll see later. If you don't need a callback, you can pass a NULL for this parameter.

The cmd parameter specifies the type of application and events the program wants to receive (see Table 4-1). For clients with no callback function you'll use

```
APPCLASS_STANDARD | APPCMD_CLIENTONLY |
CBF_SKIP_ALLNOTIFICATIONS
```

If you do have a callback, you might use

```
APPCLASS_STANDARD | APPCMD_CLIENTONLY
```

You can add CBF_SKIP commands (see Table 4-1) for any notifications you don't process. Strictly speaking, this is not necessary, but it makes your application more efficient if you don't process certain notifications.

The final parameter to DdeInitialize() is not used and should be set to zero.

Table 4-1. Common DdeInitialize Flags

Flags	Meaning
APPCLASS_STANDARD	Ordinary DDE application
APPCMD_CLIENTONLY	Fails all server transactions (used for client programs)
APPCMD_FILTERINITS	Prevents XTYP_CONNECT and XTYP_WILDCONNECT events

Callback

A client may use a DDE callback if it requires any of the following:

- Notifications of DDE servers starting or exiting
- Notifications of disconnections
- Asynchronous data transactions

If your client doesn't need any of these, you can write a dummy callback that just returns NULL or, better still, supply NULL as the pointer to the callback.

If you need a callback, here is the prototype of a typical one:

```
HDDEDATA CALLBACK DDEFunc(UINT type, UINT fmt,
                    HCONV conversation,
                    HSZ string, HDDEDATA data,
                    DWORD data1, DWORD data2)
  {
  switch (type)
    {
```

```
case XTYP_REGISTER:
case XTYP_UNREGISTER:
  /* your code here */
  break;

case XTYP_ADVDATA:
  /* your code here */
  return DDE_FACK;

case XTYP_XACT_COMPLETE:
  /* your code here */
  return NULL;
  }
return NULL;
  }
```

Table 4-2 shows the callback types that a client might handle.
Note that the return value varies depending on the callback
type.

Table 4-2. DDE Client Callback Types

Type	Description
XTYP_ADVDATA	Advises loop data changed
XTYP_DISCONNECT	Server terminated conversation
XTYP_ERROR	Critical error
XTYP_REGISTER	New server registered
XTYP_UNREGISTER	Server closing
XTYP_XACT_COMPLETE	Asynchronous transaction complete

Connection

Before a client can receive data or transmit commands, it must connect to a DDE server. The DdeConnect() function is the most common way to do this. You pass DdeConnect() your DDE instance and two string handles (see Chapter 3 for more about string handles). One string handle represents the service name, and the other is the topic. You can also pass DdeConnect(), a pointer to a CONVCONTEXT structure to handle multiple language transactions. Ordinarily, you can pass a NULL for this argument to get the default structure. DdeConnect() returns a conversation handle, which uniquely identifies the connection. You'll pass it to many other DDE functions.

You can also connect to multiple servers using DdeConnectList(), which returns an HCONVLIST list. You can then examine each conversation handle using DdeQueryNextServer().

If you can't connect to a server, you may need to start it by using WinExec(). Most, but not all, servers use their name as their service name. Therefore, if you can't connect to service WinWord, you can use WinExec() to start WinWord and try to connect again.

Finding Information

Given a conversation handle, you can find out about the conversation by calling DdeQueryConvInfo(). This function fills in a CONVINFO structure (see Table 4-3). This is especially useful if you want to construct a list of available DDE servers.

Table 4-3. The CONVINFO Structure Members

Member	Type	Description
cb	DWORD	Size of structure
hUser	DWORD	User-defined
hConvPartner	HCONV	Partner's DDEML handle (0 for non-DDEML applications)
hszSvcPartner	HSZ	Partner's name
hszServiceReq	HSZ	Service name
hszTopic	HSZ	Topic
hszItem	HSZ	Item
wFmt	UINT	Format of data
wType	UINT	Transaction type (same as received by callback)
wStatus	UINT	Status
wConvst	UINT	State of conversation
wLastError	UINT	Last error
hConvList	HCONVLIST	List that this conversation is a part of (if any)
ConvCtxt	CONVCONTEXT	Conversation context

The DDELIST program on the companion disk (see Listing 4-1) illustrates how to use DdeQueryConvInfo() to find a list of all DDE servers that support the system topic. It uses the following line to create a list of servers:

```
convlist=DdeConnectList(dde_inst,NULL,system,NULL,NULL);
```

Armed with this list, it is simple to find the server names and add them to a list box:

```
while (conv=DdeQueryNextServer(convlist,conv))
  {
  DdeQueryConvInfo(conv,QID_SYNC,&info);
  DdeQueryString(dde_inst,info.hszSvcPartner,name,
      sizeof(name),CP_WINANSI);
  SendMessage(w,LB_ADDSTRING,0,(DWORD)name);
  }
```

Listing 4-1. DDELIST.C

```
/* DDELIST -- list DDE servers that support the
   System topic */
#include <windows.h>
#include <ddeml.h>
#include "ddelist.h"

/* Program instance */
HANDLE hInst;

/* DDEML Instance */
DWORD dde_inst=0;

/* Flag dde active */
int dde_active=0;

/* List of conversations */
HCONVLIST convlist;
/* Specific conversation */
HCONV conv;


char buf[128];  /* general purpose buffer */

/* Create dialog to contain list of servers */
```

```
BOOL FAR PASCAL _export ctrl_dlg(HWND hDlg,
                          unsigned message,
                          WORD wParam, LONG lParam)
    {
    switch (message)
      {
      case WM_INITDIALOG:
/* Set up list */
          fill_box(GetDlgItem(hDlg,SERVERS));
          return TRUE;

      case WM_COMMAND:
            if (wParam==IDCANCEL)
              {
              EndDialog(hDlg,0);
              return TRUE;
              }
      }
    return FALSE;
    }

/* Start DDE and connect to all servers that support system
   topic */
dde_start()
  {
  HSZ system;
  DdeInitialize(&dde_inst,NULL,
        APPCLASS_STANDARD|APPCMD_CLIENTONLY,0);
  system=DdeCreateStringHandle(dde_inst,"SYSTEM",CP_WINANSI);
  convlist=DdeConnectList(dde_inst,NULL,system,NULL,NULL);
  DdeFreeStringHandle(dde_inst,system);
  return 0;
  }
```

```
void dde_end()
  {
   DdeDisconnectList(convlist);
  }



/* This is the workhorse function -- it finds the server
   names and puts them in the list box designated by the
   w parameter */
fill_box(HWND w)
  {
  int ct=0;
  char name[66];
  CONVINFO info;
  dde_start();   /* Start DDEML and connect to list */
  while (conv=DdeQueryNextServer(convlist,conv))
    {
/* Get info */
    DdeQueryConvInfo(conv,QID_SYNC,&info);
/* Convert handle to string */
    DdeQueryString(dde_inst,info.hszSvcPartner,name,
        sizeof(name),CP_WINANSI);
/* Update list box */
    SendMessage(w,LB_ADDSTRING,0,(DWORD)name);
    }
/* Done! */
  dde_end();
  }



/* Main window function */
int PASCAL WinMain(HANDLE hInstance, HANDLE prev,
                  LPSTR cmdline, int show)
    {
```

```
FARPROC control;
hInst=hInstance;
control=MakeProcInstance(ctrl_dlg,hInst);
DialogBox(hInst,CONTROL_DLG,NULL,control);
FreeProcInstance(control);
DdeUninitialize(dde_inst);
return FALSE;
}
```

Transactions

Client programs can use DdeClientTransaction() to request a
transaction with the server. The type of transaction depends
on what you need from the server. Here are the possible types:

- XTYP_REQUEST—This request causes the server to return
  a data item while the client waits. This is a cold link.

- XTYP_ADVSTART—When the server receives this transaction request, it begins an advise loop with the client. The
  server will send a message to the client's callback whenever
  the data item changes. This is a hot link. If you combine this
  with the XTYPF_ACKREQ constant, the server will wait for
  an acknowledgement before continuing.

- XTYP_ADVSTART | XTYPF_NODATA—This transaction
  is identical to a simple XTYP_ADVSTART, except that the
  server only notifies the client that the data changed—it
  doesn't send the data. This is a warm link.

- XTYP_ADVSTOP—The client issues this request when it
  no longer wants to receive notifications from a previous
  XTYP_ADVSTART transaction.

- XTYP_EXECUTE—The client program can send
  commands to the server with XTYP_EXECUTE. The
  format of the command depends entirely on the server.

The Windows Program Manager, for example, provides commands to create groups, add program items, and make group windows visible.

- XTYP_POKE—Some servers can accept unsolicited data from clients. This transaction sends this data to a server.

If DdeClientTransaction() returns a data handle, you must free it using DdeFreeDataHandle(). See Chapter 3 for more details about accessing data handles.

If you request a synchronous transaction, you must specify a time out value in milliseconds. DDEML returns an error if the server doesn't respond within that time.

Disconnect

When the client no longer needs a connection, it calls DdeDisconnect() or DdeDisconnectList(). This invalidates the conversation handle and frees any DDEML resources associated with that conversation. After disconnecting, the client can still form new connections without calling DdeInitialize() again.

Uninitialize

Before a client program exits, it must call DdeUninitialize(). This ends its relationship with DDEML.

An Example Program

The SUBGROUP example program (see Figure 4-1) uses DDE to extend Program Manager to use subgroups. Program Manager supports several DDE commands and data items (see the accompanying box entitled "The Program Manager DDE Interface"). SUBGROUP uses this interface to activate a group specified on its command line. When you give

Figure 4-1. SUBGROUP in Action

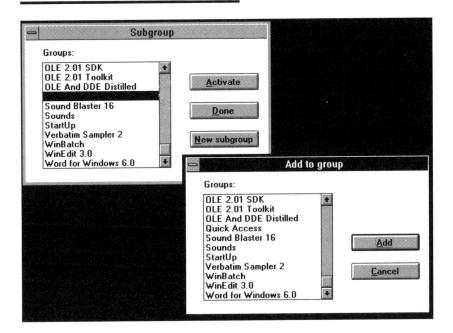

SUBGROUP an icon in a Program Manager group, it appears that the group contains a subgroup nested within.

Sending commands is a simple operation. Here is the entire activate_grp() function:

```
void activate_grp(LPSTR cmdline)
    {
    char cmd[128];
    dde_start();
    sprintf(cmd,"[ShowGroup(%Fs,2)][ShowGroup[%Fs,1]",
            cmdline,cmdline);
    dde_trans(cmd,strlen(cmd)+1,conv,NULL,0,XTYP_EXECUTE,
            10000,NULL);
    dde_end();
    }
```

The Program Manager DDE Interface

Program Manager (and other Windows shell programs) supports a DDE interface that allows other programs to control it. Many install programs take advantage of this facility to add items and groups to the Program Manager. As SUBGROUP shows, there are also other uses for it.

All transactions with Program Manager use the PROGMAN server and PROGMAN topic. If the item name is GROUPS, PROGMAN returns a list of available groups (one per line).

If the item name is the name of a group, PROGMAN returns information about that group. The following information is available on the first data line (the items are separated by commas):

- Group name (in quotation marks)
- Pathname of group file
- The number of items

Each subsequent line contains information about a particular item:

- The item's command line (in quotation marks)
- The default directory
- The icon path name
- The item's position in the group
- The icon's index
- A number that represents the item's hotkey
- The run flag (for example, normal, minimize, and so on)

Here is a typical result from a DDE request on a group:

```
"Main",C:\WINDOWS\MAIN.GRP,7,7
  "File Manager","WINFILE.EXE",
  ,C:\WINDOWS\WINFILE.EXE,
  21,0,0,0,0 "Read Me","README.WRI",
  ,write.exe,321,0,0,0,0"Control Panel",
  "CONTROL.EXE",,C:\WINDOWS\CONTROL.EXE,
  96,0,0,0,0"Windows Setup","SETUP.EXE",
  ,C:\WINDOWS\SETUP.EXE,21,72,
  0,0,0"PIF Editor","PIFEDIT.EXE",
  ,C:\WINDOWS\PIFEDIT.EXE,96,72,0,0,0
```

If you use a Program Manager replacement, it may or may not support the GROUPS and group information items.

Program Manager also supports several commands that allow you to manipulate it:

CreateGroup(name,[path])	Creates a new group with the specified name and optional group file name.
ShowGroup(name,cmd)	Display group. The cmd parameter can range from 1 to 8 (see Table 4-4).
DeleteGroup(name)	Deletes a group and its contents.
Reload([group])	Reloads a group from its group file. If you specify no group, PROGMAN reloads all groups.

AddItem(cmd, [name], [icon_file], [icon_index], [x], [y], [start_dir], [hotkey], [minimize])	Adds a new item to the current group. The parameters are as follows:

- cmd — The command line
- name — The item name
- icon_file — The file that contains the item's icon
- icon_index — Which icon to use from the icon_file
- x — The new item's X coordinate (horizontal position). If this parameter is present, the y parameter is not optional
- y — The new item's Y coordinate (vertical position)
- start_dir — The working directory
- hotkey — The item's shortcut key
- minimize — The item's run state

DeleteItem(item)	Removes item from current group.
ReplaceItem(item)	Removes item from current group and marks its position for use by the next AddItem command.
ExitProgMan(save)	Exits program manager. The save parameter specifies if PROGMAN saves its current state. If PROGMAN is your default shell, this command won't work.

Table 4-4. ShowGroup Parameters

Value	Meaning
1	Activates and displays the group window
2	Activates the group as an icon
3	Activates and maximizes the group window
4	Restores window
5	Activates window in place
6	Minimizes window
7	Displays as icon

The dde_start() (see Listing 4-2) and dde_end() functions establish the conversation. SUBGROUP's dde_trans() function is a simple wrapper around DdeClientTransaction() that provides a message box when an error occurs. Otherwise, it is identical to DdeClientTransaction().

Listing 4-2. Connecting to Program Manager

```
/* Start up DDEML with PROGMAN/PROGMAN conversation */
dde_start()
  {
  HSZ progman;
  DdeInitialize(&dde_inst,NULL,
      APPCLASS_STANDARD|APPCMD_CLIENTONLY,0);
  progman=DdeCreateStringHandle(dde_inst,
      "PROGMAN",CP_WINANSI);
  conv=DdeConnect(dde_inst,progman,progman,NULL);
  DdeFreeStringHandle(dde_inst,progman);
  return 0;
  }
```

If you run SUBGROUP with no parameters, you can automatically install a subgroup icon in a Program Manager group. To do this, SUBGROUP issues an XTYP_REQUEST to Program Manager to obtain a list of available groups (see Listing 4-3). It uses the DdeAccessData() function to get a pointer to the group names and places them in the list box. Once SUBGROUP finishes with the data, it calls DdeUnaccessData() and DdeFreeDataHandle() to release resources.

Listing 4-3. Finding Group Names

```
/* Fill box with group names */
void fill_box(HWND w)
  {
  HSZ group;
  HDDEDATA data;
  DWORD size;
  char far *p,far *st;
  dde_start();
/* Ask for groups item */
  group=DdeCreateStringHandle(dde_inst,"GROUPS",
        CP_WINANSI);
  data=dde_trans(NULL,0,conv,group,CF_TEXT,XTYP_REQUEST,
        10000,NULL);
  st=p=DdeAccessData(data,&size);
/* Parse group names from list */
  while (*p)
    {
    while (*p&&*p!='\r') p++;
    if (*p)
      {
      *p='\0';
      SendMessage(w,LB_ADDSTRING,0,(DWORD)st);
```

```
        st=p=p+2;   /* skip cr & lf */
        }
    }
DdeUnaccessData(data);
DdeFreeDataHandle(data);
DdeFreeStringHandle(dde_inst,group);
dde_end();
}
```

Summary

DDE clients need not be complicated. Using XTYP_REQUEST transactions to establish cold links is not difficult; warm and hot links are only slightly more difficult. Using DDE to issue commands to servers is also very simple. With DDEML, there is no reason to exclude DDE support from your applications.

5

At Your Service— Writing DDE Servers

WHAT'S IN THIS CHAPTER

This chapter shows how to write DDE servers. It also presents a library that greatly simplifies the creation of most servers.

PREREQUISITES

Understanding of Windows programming, clipboard formats, and DDE concepts.

DDE servers provide data to clients. They can also accept commands (as PROGMAN does) and take unsolicited data (via pokes). Although DDEML simplifies writing both clients and servers, it is more difficult to write a server. However, if you are adding server functionality to an existing application, you'll find that the server's code is largely self-contained. You'll need to write routines to access your application's data, but you won't have to modify much of your existing code.

Server Responsibilities

Most servers provide only one service name, which usually matches the server's program name. This simplifies things for clients that need to start your server since they may use the service name as an argument to WinExec().

Servers should support the SYSTEM topic (see Chapter 3). Many programs that attempt to locate servers require the SYSTEM topic. Any application can use the SYSTEM topic to learn what items and formats your server supports.

Server Processing

Most server processing is done in the DDE callback (see Listing 5-1). A basic server initializes DDEML, handles messages via its DDE callback, and terminates.

Listing 5-1. Typical DDE Server Callback

```
HDDEDATA FAR PASCAL _export dde_cb(UINT type,UINT fmt,
   HCONV conv, HSZ hsz1, HSZ hsz2, HDDEDATA data,
   DWORD data1,DWORD data2)
   {
   switch (type)
```

```
    {
    case XTYP_ERROR:        /* error */
        {
        /* Error handling */
        break;
        }

    case XTYP_ADVREQ:       /* Send data to advise loop */
// if string handle is "SYSTEM" call do_system
        if (!DdeCmpStringHandles(hsz1,system))
          return do_system(hsz2);
// if string handle is "TOPIC1" call do_topic
        if (!DdeCmpStringHandles(hsz1,topic1))
          return do_topic(hsz2);
        break;

    case XTYP_ADVSTART:     /* Begin advise loop */
// if string handle is "TOPIC1" accept advise loop
        if (!DdeCmpStringHandles(hsz1,topic1)) return 1;
// if string handle is "SYSTEM" and good item  accept
        if (!DdeCmpStringHandles(hsz1,system))
          {
          int i;
          for (i=0;i<sizeof(sysitems)/sizeof(sysitems[0]);i++)
            if (!DdeCmpStringHandles(hsz2,sysitems[i]))
              return 1;
          }
// reject advise loop
        return 0;

    case XTYP_ADVSTOP:   /* End of advise loop */
// don't care
```

```
        break;

    case XTYP_CONNECT:    /* Connect */
        return (!DdeCmpStringHandles(topic1,hsz1)
                ||!DdeCmpStringHandles(system,hsz1))&&
                !DdeCmpStringHandles(service,hsz2);
        break;

    case XTYP_CONNECT_CONFIRM:    /* confirmation of connect */
// no special action here for this server
        break;

    case XTYP_DISCONNECT:    /* Disconnect */
// this server doesn't care
        break;

    case XTYP_EXECUTE:    /* Execute */
// not used by this server
        break;

    case XTYP_POKE:    /* Poke data */
// not used
        break;
    case XTYP_REQUEST:    /* Cold data request */
        if (!DdeCmpStringHandles(hsz1,system))
          return do_system(hsz2);
        if (!DdeCmpStringHandles(hsz1,topic1)
          return do_topic(hsz2);
        break;

    case XTYP_WILDCONNECT:  /* Wild connect */
        {
```

```
        HSZPAIR connects[3];
        if (hsz2&&DdeCmpStringHandles(hsz2,service)) return NULL;
        if (!hsz1)
          {
          /* return HSZPAIR of all topics */
          connects[1].hszSvc=connects[0].hszSvc=server;
          connects[0].hszTopic=system;
          connects[1].hszTopic=topic1;
          connects[2].hszSvc=connects[2].hszTopic=NULL;
          }
        else if (!DdeCmpStringHandles(hsz1,system))
          {
          connects[0].hszSvc=service;
          connects[0].hszTopic=system;
          connects[1].hszSvc=connects[1].hszTopic=NULL;
          }
        else if (!DdeCmpStringHandles(hsz1,topic1))
          {
          connects[0].hszSvc=service;
          connects[0].hszTopic=topic1;
          connects[1].hszSvc=connects[1].hszTopic=NULL;
          }
        else
          return NULL;
/* It is crucial that the data handle have an item of NULL */
        return
DdeCreateDataHandle(dde_inst,connects,sizeof(connects),
          0,NULL,0,0);
        }
    }
    return NULL;
    }
```

Initializing the server is relatively simple, requiring only a few steps (see Table 5-1 for a list of server-related DDE calls):

1. Create a procedure instance for your DDE callback (if you use the smart callbacks available with some compilers, you may omit this step).

2. Call DdeInitialize().

3. Create string handles that you need (service name, topic names, and so on).

4. Register your service name with DdeNameService().

Table 5-1. Server-Related DDEML Calls

Function	Description
DdeDisconnect()	Disconnects conversation
DdeEnableCallback()	Disables or enables transactions
DdeNameService()	Register and unregister service names
DdePostAdvise()	Notifies DDEML that data has changed

Your DDE callback must handle several transaction types (see Table 5-2). Of course, you can omit some of these types if you don't need full server functionality. For example, if you don't allow wild card connections, you don't need to process XTYP_WILDCONNECT or XTYP_CONNECTCONFIRM transactions. Likewise, if you don't allow hot or warm links, you can safely not process the XTYP_ADVSTART, XTYP_ADVREQ, and XTYP_ADVSTOP transactions.

If you don't support certain transactions, you can ask DDEML to filter them when you call DdeInitialize(). For example, specifying the CBF_FAIL_POKES flag prevents you from receiving XTYP_POKE transactions. See Table 5-3 for a list of filters available.

Table 5-2. Server Transactions

Transaction	Description
XTYP_CONNECT	Client requests connection
XTYP_WILDCONNECT	Client requests connection with wildcards
XTYP_CONNECT_CONFIRM	Client confirms connection
XTYP_DISCONNECT	Client disconnected
XTYP_REQUEST	Processes client request
XTYP_ADVSTART	Starts advise loop
XTYP_ADVREQ	Advises loop data changed
XTYP_ADVSTOP	Ends advise loop
XTYP_EXECUTE	Processes command
XTYP_POKE	Processes poke (unsolicited) data

Table 5-3. DDEML Server Filters

Filter	Meaning
CBF_FAIL_ADVISES	Fails XTYP_ADVSTART and XTYP_ADVSTOP
CBF_FAIL_CONNECTIONS	Fails XTYP_CONNECT and XTYP_WILDCONNECT
CBF_FAIL_EXECUTES	Fails XTYP_EXECUTE
CBF_FAIL_POKES	Fails XTYP_POKE
CBF_FAIL_REQUESTS	Fails XTYP_REQUEST
CBF_SKIP_CONNECT_CONFIRMS	Prevents XTYP_CONNECT_CONFIRMS
CBF_SKIP_SELFCONNECTIONS	Denies connections from the same program instance
CBF_SKIP_DISCONNECTS	Inhibits XTYP_DISCONNECTION

When a DDE item changes, you must call DdePostAdvise(). This causes DDEML to automatically update any hot and warm links outstanding on that item. You can also call DdePostAdvise() with a NULL argument to force DDEML to update all outstanding links.

Once you are ready to terminate, you essentially reverse the above steps:

1. Unregister your service name with DdeNameService().

2. Free any string handles you created.

3. Call DdeUninitialize().

4. Free your callback procedure instance, if you created one.

Managing Connections

Once you register your service name, DDEML sends you either a XTYP_CONNECT message when a client requests a conversation with you or a XTYP_WILDCONNECT message if it requests a conversation with anyone.

Ordinary Connections

When you receive an XTYP_CONNECT transaction, you can examine the two string handles DDEML passes to your callback. The first string is the topic name and the second is the service name. If these string handles match a service and topic that you support, you return TRUE; otherwise, return FALSE to deny the connection. When comparing string handles, make sure to use DdeCmpStringHandles() so that the comparison won't be case-sensitive.

Wild Connections

XTYP_WILDCONNECT transactions are more difficult to process. The parameters are the same as an XTYP_CONNECT, but one or both of the string handles may be NULL. To allow connections, you must create a data handle (see Chapter 3) that contains an array of HSZPAIR structures. Each element of the array specifies a service and topic name that matches the wild connect request. The array ends with a NULL entry.

Instead of building this array and then creating a data handle, it is often easier to create an empty data handle and then fill it with the array elements. Here is a code fragment that shows how:

```
/* nrtopics is total number of topics, topics[] is array of
   string handles, and server is string handle of server name */
int i,offset=0;
data=DdeCreateDataHandle(dde_inst,NULL,
                         nrtopics*sizeof(HSZPAIR),0,
                         NULL,0,0);
for (i=0;i<nrtopics;i++)
  {
  HSZPAIR con;
  con.hszSvc=server;
  con.hszTopic=topics[i];
  DdeAddData(data,&con,sizeof(con),offset);
  offset+=sizeof(con);
  }
```

Connect Confirmation

Once a client successfully connects with your server, you will receive a XTYP_CONNECT_CONFIRM transaction. This allows you to store the conversation handle if you need it. If you don't need to process this transaction, specify CBF_SKIP_CONNECT_CONFIRMS in your call to DdeInitialize().

Disconnect

If the client disconnects from your server, your callback receives a XTYP_DISCONNECT message, which allows you to clean up any resources you allocated to support the conversation. If you don't need this transaction, pass the CBF_SKIP_DISCONNECTS flag to DdeInitialize().

Managing Data

Client requests enter your callback function as XTYP_-REQUEST transactions. The data you return to the client is in the form of a data handle (see Chapter 3). You use DdeCreateDataHandle() to create a handle. You can initialize the handle with data or fill it in later using DdeAccessData() or DdeAddData() (see Chapter 3 for more on data handles).

When you call DdeCreateDataHandle(), you must specify a string handle that corresponds to the item name that the data represents. This is used only when the data handle is a DDE item.

If you specify HDATA_APPOWNED as the last parameter to DdeCreateDataHandle(), you may send the handle to multiple clients. Otherwise, once you send the handle to a client, you may not use it again. If you do specify HDATA_APPOWNED, you must free the handle eventually.

Warm and Hot Links

When a client requests a hot or warm link, it enters into an advise loop with the server. You receive an XTYP_ADVSTART transaction in the beginning. You can examine the topic and item (the two string handle arguments to the callback). If these string handles match a topic and item you can supply, you should return TRUE from the callback. Otherwise, return FALSE to deny the advise loop.

When DDE-accessible data in your application changes, you must call DdePostAdvise(). If there are active advise loops for the data, DDEML sends your callback an XTYP_ADVREQ for each loop. This transaction is very similar to an XTYP_REQUEST transaction. You simply build a data handle and return it.

When the client ends a warm or hot link, your callback receives an XTYP_ADVSTOP transaction. You can free any resources you used to satisfy the advise loop.

Supporting the SYSTEM Topic

The SYSTEM topic (see Chapter 3) is no different from any other topic. You simply build a string to satisfy the request, place it into a data handle, and return it to the client. DDEML doesn't afford the SYSTEM topic any special treatment.

A Server Library

If you examine Listing 5-1 (earlier in this chapter), you might notice that much of the server's callback is repetitive but not overly complex. Since so much of a DDE server repeats itself, you can easily write a DDE server engine that operates with tables to define topics and items.

The DDESRV library (see Listing 5-2 at the end of this chapter) does just this. By setting up some tables and writing a few functions to create data handles, you can easily create a DDE server. You need only a few calls to start the library; call DdePostAdvise() when you change DDE data.

Data Types

When you use DDESRV, you must set up an array of TOPIC items. These items contain a string handle (the topic's name) and a pointer to an array of type ITEM. The ITEM array for each topic contains a string handle (the item's name), a type, and a clipboard format. Each element also contains an action union. This union may contain a string, a data buffer, a data handle, or a pointer to a function that returns a data handle. The type field determines what is in the union. Table 5-4 shows the data types allowed.

Table 5-4. DDESRV Data Types

Type	Description
TYPE_STRING	Ordinary C string
TYPE_DATA	DDESRV DATA type
TYPE_FUNC	User-defined function
TYPE_DDEDATA	DDE data handle
TYPE_END	End of ITEM array

The action union determines what data a particular topic and item returns. If it contains a string or data buffer, DDESRV automatically creates the necessary data handles. The clipboard format field is used only when handling a data buffer. Once initialized, DDESRV automatically searches the list of topics and items to satisfy DDE requests.

As a special case, any item with a string handle equal to NO_HSZ (defined in DDESTRNG.H) will match any DDE request. This allows you to pass control to a function that can decide how to service the item. If you have varying items, this may be easier than reconstructing the ITEM array dynamically.

Often DDESTRNG is useful in conjunction with DDESRV (see DDESTRNG.C on the companion disk). This library provides a DDESTRING type that contains a character pointer and a string handle. You may initialize an array of type DDESTRING with character strings and pass it to the mk_stringhandles() function. The function fills in the correct string handles. When you are done with them, you can pass the array to free_stringhandles() to free the string handles. DDESTRNG supplies a global variable (codepage) that sets the string handle's code page. By default this is CP_WINANSI, but you may change this if you like.

DDESRV does not use any functions from DDESTRNG, although it provides a call to initialize your TOPIC and ITEM arrays from a DDESTRING array (the example server in this chapter does this). Although this is not necessary, it is often more convenient then setting it up manually. DDESRV also needs the definition for NO_HSZ found in DDESTRNG.H.

Using the Server Library

There are only five steps you must perform to set up the server:

1. Call server_init() with your instance handle as an argument (see Table 5-5 for a complete list of DDESRV calls). Save the instance handle it returns for later use.

2. Create the string handles your server requires. You'll need one for your service name and one for each topic. You also need a string handle for most items that you support. However, by using a NO_HSZ string handle in your ITEM table, you can act on any item without specifically generating a string handle for it. You can use the mk_stringhandles() call to convert an array of strings into string handles.

3. Create and fill in the TOPIC and ITEM arrays using the string handles you made in the previous step. Later, you will learn how to use server_fill() to simplify this step in some cases.

4. Use server_setexec(), server_seterr(), and server_setpoke() to set callbacks for errors, execute commands, and pokes, if desired. If you want to use the default handlers, you don't need to do this step.

5. Call server() with your service name string handle and the address of your TOPIC table.

Table 5-5. DDESRV Calls

Call	Meaning
server_init()	Initializes DDESRV
server()	Begins server operation
sserver_fill()	Initializes TOPIC and ITEM arrays from string table
server_seterr()	Sets error function
server_setexec()	Sets execute function
server_setpoke()	Sets poke function
server_end()	Terminates server operations
server_done()	Ends DDESRV

Once you call server(), you are in the DDE server business. For items that have the TYPE_STRING, TYPE_DATA, or TYPE_DDEDATA attributes, the server library automatically satisfies data requests. If the attribute is TYPE_FUNC, the library will call the specified function to provide data. This function accepts two data handles (the topic and item names) and must return a data handle.

When you are ready to terminate, call server_end(). This shuts down your server but does not end your DDEML session. You can then free your string handles before calling server_done() to completely end your DDEML session. If you used mk_stringhandles(), you can free the string table with free_stringhandles().

Advising Data

As in a normal DDE server, you must notify DDEML when a data item changes. This allows DDEML to satisfy any outstanding warm or hot links. When an item changes, simply call DdePostAdvise() using the DDE handle (from the server_init() function) and string handles to specify the topic and item that changed.

User-defined Functions

By using server_seterr(), server_setexec(), and server_-setpoke(), you can set functions to handle errors, execute commands, and pokes, respectively. If you fail to set an error function (or set it to NULL), the server library provides a default. The default execute and poke handlers do nothing.

Your error function has no return value and receives the DDE error code as an argument. The execute and poke functions return DDE_FACK if successful, DDE_FNOTPROCESSED if unsuccessful, and DDE_FBUSY if busy. The execute function receives the topic's string handle and a far character pointer to the command. The poke function receives two string handles (the topic and item) and a data handle.

DDESRV Shortcuts

DDESRV offers several shortcuts that can simplify many servers. If you use the DDESTRNG library to create a table of string handles, you can pass the table to server_fill() to automatically fill in your TOPIC and ITEM tables. In the string table, each topic must be followed immediately by its items. If you have a wild-card entry in the item table (to match any item), you must have a NO_HSZ entry in the string table. Here is a typical example:

```
DDESTRING str[]=
  {
    {NULL,"USERINFO"},       /* first topic */
    {NO_HSZ,NULL},           /* null entry */
    {NULL,SZDDESYS_TOPIC},   /* second topic */
    {NULL,SZDDESYS_ITEM_FORMATS},
    {NULL,SZDDESYS_ITEM_STATUS},
    {NULL,SZDDESYS_ITEM_TOPICS},
    {NULL,SZDDESYS_ITEM_SYSITEMS},
    {NULL,NULL}              /* end of table */
  };
```

When you build your string table, you may want to put other strings (the service name, for example) ahead of the topic and item strings. If you do this, simply add an offset to the call to server_fill(). For example, if you had this table,

```
DDESTRING str[]=
  {
    {NULL,"LOGIN"},          /* Server name */
    {NULL,"USERINFO"},       /* first topic */
    {NO_HSZ,NULL},           /* null entry */
    {NULL,SZDDESYS_TOPIC},   /* second topic */
    {NULL,SZDDESYS_ITEM_FORMATS},
    {NULL,SZDDESYS_ITEM_STATUS},
    {NULL,SZDDESYS_ITEM_TOPICS},
```

```
    {NULL,SZDDESYS_ITEM_SYSITEMS},
    {NULL,NULL}                    /* end of table */
  };
```

you could call server_fill() like this:

```
server_fill(topic,str+1);
```

Another way to simplify your server is to use DDESRV's built-in item handlers. Table 5-6 shows the predefined item handlers available. The server_sysfmts() function returns only CF_TEXT as an available format. If you support other formats, you won't be able to use it. The server_items() function returns all available items for a topic (unless you use a NULL item to match all items). This is useful in the SYSTEM topic or in other topics. To use the predefined functions, just place them in your ITEM table with a type of TYPE_FUNC.

Table 5-6. DDESRV Predefined Item Handlers

Function	Item
server_sysfmts()	SZDDESYS_ITEM_FORMATS
server_sysstatus()	SZDDESYS_ITEM_STATUS
server_systopics()	SZDDESYS_ITEM_TOPICS
server_items()	SZDDE_ITEM_ITEMLIST

An Example Server

LOGIN.C (see Listing 5-3 at the end of this chapter and Figure 5-1) is a complete DDE server that uses DDESRV. This server provides a dialog box that contains an item for each entry in the LOGIN.INI file (see Listing 5-4). When a client asks for an item in the USERINFO topic, LOGIN searches the LOGIN.INI

Figure 5-1. The LOGIN DDE Server

file using the currently selected section (from the dialog) and the ITEM name. If the entry exists in the INI file, LOGIN returns the resulting string to the client. Otherwise, LOGIN returns the string "N/A".

If a client requests USERINFO,EXTENSION it will get the string "109" or "101" depending on the current selection in the LOGIN dialog box (see Listing 5-4). The LOGINDOC.WBT file on the companion disk is a WINBATCH script that uses LOGIN. A shareware copy of WINBATCH (from Wilson WindowWare) is also on the companion disk.

Notice that LOGIN uses a wild card in the ITEM array since the specific items can change depending on the current user. If there are some fixed items, you can put them before the NULL entry in the ITEM table since DDESRV searches the table sequentially. The NULL entry is then the last resort for matching items in the USERINFO topic.

LOGIN also accepts execute commands. If you pass a user name enclosed in square brackets, LOGIN uses it to set the current user.

Listing 5-4. LOGIN.INI

```
[Patrick Williams]
Name=Patrick A. Williams
Title=Associate
Extension=109

[Scott Anderson]
Name=J. S. Anderson
Title=Stellar Training
Extension=101
```

Summary

DDE servers are certainly more complex to write than clients. This is especially true if you implement the SYSTEM topic properly (and you should). However, with DDEML and DDESVR, you can write most servers without much difficulty.

You can use DDE to communicate with a variety of programs (as LOGIN does) or to establish realtime data conduits between multiple programs that cooperate. For example, if you write a program to collect temperature data from an instrument, you can send the data using DDE to your display and graphing software.

In later chapters, you'll see how you can use OLE to replace DDE in some situations. However, for simple applications that need only DDE communications, this is often more trouble than it is worth.

Listing 5-2. DDESRV.C

```c
/* DDE Server Library -- Williams */
#include "ddesrv.h"
#include <string.h>


/* various static variables */
static DWORD dde_inst;
static HSZ servername;
static TOPIC *servertopics;
static void (*errfunc)(int)=server_errfunc;
static DWORD (*execfunc)(HSZ,char _far *);
static DWORD (*pokefunc)(HSZ,HSZ,HDDEDATA);
static FARPROC ddecb;


/* Service data requests */
static HDDEDATA data_req(HSZ hsz1,HSZ hsz2)
  {
  int i,j;
  HDDEDATA rv=NULL;
/* Find topic */
  for (i=0;servertopics[i].topic;i++)
    if (!DdeCmpStringHandles(servertopics[i].topic,hsz1))
      {
/* find item */
      for (j=0;servertopics[i].items[j].type!=TYPE_END;j++)
        if (servertopics[i].items[j].item==NO_HSZ||
           !DdeCmpStringHandles(servertopics[i].items[j].
             item,hsz2))
          {
/* Process according to type */
          switch (servertopics[i].items[j].type)
            {
```

```
            case TYPE_STRING:
/* Move fixed string to data handle */
            rv=DdeCreateDataHandle(dde_inst,
            servertopics[i].items[j].action.str,
                strlen(servertopics[i].items[j].action.str)+1,
                0,hsz2,CF_TEXT,0);
            break;

            case TYPE_FUNC:
/* Call user function */
            rv=(*servertopics[i].items[j].action.fn)(hsz1,
                hsz2);
            break;

            case TYPE_DDEDATA:
/* return DDE data */
            rv=servertopics[i].items[j].action.ddedata;
            break;

            case TYPE_DATA:
/* DATA (buffer,length) to data handle */
            rv=DdeCreateDataHandle(dde_inst,
                servertopics[i].items[j].action.data->p,
                servertopics[i].items[j].action.data->len
                ,0,hsz2,
                servertopics[i].items[j].fmt,0);
            break;
        }
        return rv;  /* return whatever was needed */
        }
    }
/* Not found; return NULL */
```

```
    return NULL;
    }



/* Callback */
HDDEDATA FAR PASCAL _export dde_cbk(UINT type,UINT fmt,
                        HCONV conv, HSZ hsz1, HSZ hsz2,
                        HDDEDATA data,DWORD data1,
                        DWORD data2)
    {
    int i;
    switch (type)
      {
      case XTYP_ERROR:
          {
/* Call user's error function */
          if (errfunc)
            errfunc(LOWORD(data1));
          break;
          }


      case XTYP_ADVSTART:
/* Start advise loop if topic/item found, if a wildcard
   entry is found in the item list, allow loop */
        for (i=0;servertopics[i].topic;i++)
          if (!DdeCmpStringHandles(servertopics[i].topic,
                            hsz1))
            {
            int j;
            for (j=0;servertopics[i].items[j].type!=TYPE_END
                  ;j++)
              if (servertopics[i].items[j].item==NO_HSZ||
```

```
                        !DdeCmpStringHandles(
                            servertopics[i].items[j].item,hsz2))
                      return 1;
                  }
              return 0;


        case XTYP_ADVREQ:
        case XTYP_REQUEST:
/* Return data */
                return data_req(hsz1,hsz2);


        case XTYP_CONNECT:
                if (!DdeCmpStringHandles(servername,hsz2))
                  {
                  /* Found server */
                  for (i=0;servertopics[i].topic;i++)
                    if (!DdeCmpStringHandles(
                            servertopics[i].topic,hsz1))
                        return 1;
                  }
              return 0;


        case XTYP_EXECUTE:
            if (execfunc)
              {
              char _far *s;
              DWORD rv;
              s=DdeAccessData(data,NULL);
              rv=execfunc(hsz1,s);
              DdeUnaccessData(data);
              return rv;
              }
```

```
      return DDE_FNOTPROCESSED;



case XTYP_POKE:
     if (pokefunc)
       return pokefunc(hsz1,hsz2,data);
     else
       return DDE_FNOTPROCESSED;


case XTYP_WILDCONNECT:
        if (!hsz2||!DdeCmpStringHandles(servername,hsz2))
          {
          /* Found server */
          if (hsz1)
            {
            HSZPAIR con[2];
            for (i=0;servertopics[i].topic;i++)
              if (!DdeCmpStringHandles(
                     servertopics[i].topic,hsz1))
                {
                con[0].hszTopic=hsz1;
                con[0].hszSvc=servername;
                con[1].hszTopic=con[1].hszSvc=NULL;
                return DdeCreateDataHandle(dde_inst,con,
                        sizeof(con),0,NULL,0,0);
                }
            }
          else
            {
            HDDEDATA data;
            int nrtopics,offset=0;
            for (nrtopics=0;
```

```
                              servertopics[nrtopics].topic;
                              nrtopics++);
                      data=DdeCreateDataHandle(dde_inst,NULL,
                              nrtopics*sizeof(HSZPAIR),
                              0,NULL,0,0);
/* Build list */
                      for (nrtopics=0
                              ;servertopics[nrtopics].topic
                              ;nrtopics++)
                          {
                          HSZPAIR con;
                          con.hszSvc=servername;
                          con.hszTopic=servertopics[nrtopics].topic;
                          DdeAddData(data,&con,sizeof(con),offset);
                          offset+=sizeof(con);
                          }
                      return data;
                      }
                  }
              return 0;
          }
      return NULL;
      }


/* Set up to go */
DWORD server_init(HINSTANCE hInst)
  {
  ddecb=MakeProcInstance((FARPROC)dde_cbk,hInst);
  if (DdeInitialize(&dde_inst,(PFNCALLBACK)ddecb,
        APPCLASS_STANDARD|CBF_SKIP_ALLNOTIFICATIONS,
        0)
          ==DMLERR_NO_ERROR) return dde_inst;
```

```
   return dde_inst;
   }


/* Start server */
DWORD server(HSZ name,TOPIC *svrs)
  {
  servertopics=svrs;
  servername=name;
  return DdeNameService(dde_inst,name,NULL,DNS_REGISTER);
  }


/* End server */
void server_end()
  {
  DdeNameService(dde_inst,servername,NULL,DNS_UNREGISTER);
  }


/* End processing */
void server_done()
  {
  FreeProcInstance(ddecb);
  DdeUninitialize(dde_inst);
  }


/* Set up arrays from String table */
void server_fill(TOPIC *topics,DDESTRING *str)
  {
  ITEM *it;
  while (topics->items&&str->hsz)
    {
    topics->topic=str->hsz;
    str++;
```

```
    it=topics->items;
    while (it->type!=TYPE_END&&str->hsz)
      {
      it->item=str->hsz;
      it++;
      str++;
      }
    topics++;
    }
  }


/* System topic helpers */
HDDEDATA server_sysfmts(HSZ hsz1,HSZ hsz2)
  {
  return DdeCreateDataHandle(dde_inst,"CF_TEXT",
            8,0,hsz2,CF_TEXT,0);
  }


HDDEDATA server_sysstatus(HSZ hsz1,HSZ hsz2)
  {
  return DdeCreateDataHandle(dde_inst,"READY",6,0,
            hsz2,CF_TEXT,0);
  }


HDDEDATA server_systopics(HSZ hsz1,HSZ hsz2)
  {
  HDDEDATA rv;
  char name[128];
  int i,offset=0;
  /* Create Handle */
  rv=DdeCreateDataHandle(dde_inst,NULL,2048,0,hsz2,
```

```
              CF_TEXT,0);
  /* Add each topic to handle */
  for (i=0;servertopics[i].topic;i++)
    {
    int l;
    l=DdeQueryString(dde_inst,servertopics[i].topic,
                       name,sizeof(name),codepage);
    if (i!=0) DdeAddData(rv,"\t",1,offset++);
    DdeAddData(rv,name,l+1,offset);
    offset+=l;
    }
  return rv;
  }


HDDEDATA server_items(HSZ hsz1,HSZ hsz2)
  {
  int i,j,offset=0;
  HDDEDATA rv;
  char name[128];
/* Scan topics */
  for (i=0;servertopics[i].topic;i++)
    {
    if (!DdeCmpStringHandles(hsz1,servertopics[i].topic))
      {
      rv=DdeCreateDataHandle(dde_inst,NULL,2048,0,
               hsz2,CF_TEXT,0);
/* Scan items */
      for (j=0;servertopics[i].items[j].type!=TYPE_END;j++)
        {
        int l;
        l=DdeQueryString(dde_inst,
               servertopics[i].items[j].item,name,
```

```
                sizeof(name),codepage);
/* Add item to list */
        if (j!=0)
            DdeAddData(rv,"\t",1,offset++);
        DdeAddData(rv,name,l+1,offset);
        offset+=l;
        }
     return rv;
     }
   }
 return NULL;
 }


void server_errfunc(int code)
  {
  char errmsg[33];
  wsprintf(errmsg,"Error %d",code);
  MessageBox(NULL,errmsg,"DDE Server Error",
            MB_OK|MB_ICONSTOP);
  }


void (*server_seterr(void (*f)(int)))(int)
  {
  void (*old)(int)=errfunc;
  errfunc=f?f:server_errfunc;
  return old;
  }


DWORD (*server_setexec(DWORD (*f)(HSZ,char _far *)))
        (HSZ,char _far *)
  {
  DWORD (*old)(HSZ,char _far *)=execfunc;
```

```
    execfunc=f;
    return old;
    }


DWORD (*server_setpoke(DWORD (*f)(HSZ,HSZ,HDDEDATA)))
        (HSZ,HSZ,HDDEDATA)
    {
    DWORD (*old)(HSZ,HSZ,HDDEDATA)=pokefunc;
    pokefunc=f;
    return old;
    }
```

Listing 5-3. LOGIN.C

```
/* LOGIN DDE Server */
#include "ddesrv.h"
#include "login.h"
#include <stdio.h>
#include <string.h>
#include <ctype.h>


HANDLE hInst;
DWORD dde_inst=0;


/* Current user */
int current=0;
/* String table */
DDESTRING str[]=
  {
    {NULL,"LOGIN"},
    {NULL,"USERINFO"},
    {NO_HSZ,NULL},
```

```
    {NULL,SZDDESYS_TOPIC},
    {NULL,SZDDESYS_ITEM_FORMATS},
    {NULL,SZDDESYS_ITEM_STATUS},
    {NULL,SZDDESYS_ITEM_TOPICS},
    {NULL,SZDDESYS_ITEM_SYSITEMS},
    {NULL,NULL}
  };

#define LOGIN str[0].hsz
#define USERINFO str[1].hsz
#define SYSTEM str[2].hsz
#define SYSFORMATS str[3].hsz
#define SYSSTATUS str[4].hsz
#define SYSITEMS str[5].hsz
#define SYSTOPICS str[6].hsz

ITEM useritems[]=
  {
  {0,TYPE_FUNC,0,do_user},
  {0,TYPE_END,0,NULL}
  };

ITEM sysitems[]=
  {
    {0,TYPE_FUNC,0,server_sysfmts},
    {0,TYPE_FUNC,0,server_sysstatus},
    {0,TYPE_FUNC,0,server_systopics},
    {0,TYPE_FUNC,0,server_items},
    {0,TYPE_END,0,NULL }
  };
```

```
TOPIC logintopics[]=
  {
    {0,useritems},
    {0,sysitems},
    {0,NULL}
  };


HWND dialog;



BOOL FAR PASCAL _export main_dlg(HWND hDlg,
                      unsigned message,
                      WORD wParam, LONG lParam)
    {
    switch (message)
      {
      case WM_INITDIALOG:
          dialog=hDlg;
          fill_box(GetDlgItem(hDlg,USERS));
          SendDlgItemMessage(hDlg,USERS,
              LB_SETCURSEL,current,0);
          return 0;


      case WM_COMMAND:
            if (wParam==IDCANCEL)
              {
              if (MessageBox(NULL,
                "Closing LOGIN will make the user"
                " information unavailable.\nDo you"
                " really want to close?",
                "Warning!",MB_YESNO|MB_ICONHAND)==IDYES)
                    EndDialog(hDlg,0);
```

```
                   return TRUE;
                   }
   // on change post advise and change current user
              if (wParam==USERS&&
                 HIWORD(lParam)==LBN_SELCHANGE)
              {
              current=SendDlgItemMessage(hDlg,USERS,
                              LB_GETCURSEL,0,0);
              DdePostAdvise(dde_inst,USERINFO,NULL);
              }
   }
   return FALSE;
   }



/* Helper function for fill_box */
void add2box(char *n,DWORD w)
  {
  SendMessage((HWND)w,LB_ADDSTRING,0,(DWORD)n);
  }



/* Call enumini to walk INI file and call add2box() */
fill_box(HWND w)
  {
  enumini("LOGIN.INI",add2box,(DWORD)w);
  }

enumini(char *fn,void (*fnc)(char *,DWORD),DWORD xtra)
  {
  char windir[66];
  int n;
```

```
  FILE *f;
  char ln[128];
  n=GetWindowsDirectory(windir,sizeof(windir));
  if (windir[n-1]!='\\') strcat(windir,"\\");
  strcat(windir,fn);
/* Open INI file */
  f=fopen(windir,"r");
  if (!f) return 0;
/* Scan lines */
  while (fgets(ln,sizeof(ln),f))
    {
    char *t=ln,*p;
    while (isspace(*t)) t++;
    if (t&&*t!='[') continue;
    p=strchr(t,']');
    if (p) *p='\0';
/* Call function */
    fnc(t+1,xtra);
    }
  fclose(f);
  return 1;
  }


/* Execute command */
DWORD docmd(HSZ topic,char _far *line)
  {
  int n;
  char _far *p;
  while (*line++!='[');
  for (p=line;*p&&*p!=']';p++);
  *p='\0';
  n=SendDlgItemMessage(dialog,USERS,
```

```
                    LB_FINDSTRINGEXACT,-1,line);
  if (n!=LB_ERR)
    {
    SendDlgItemMessage(dialog,USERS,LB_SETCURSEL,n,0);
    DdePostAdvise(dde_inst,USERINFO,NULL);
    return DDE_FACK;
    }
  return DDE_FNOTPROCESSED;
  }


/* Main window function */
int PASCAL WinMain(HANDLE hInstance, HANDLE prev,
                   LPSTR cmdline, int show)
    {
    FARPROC main;
    hInst=hInstance;
/* Start DDESRV */
    dde_inst=server_init(hInstance);
/* Fill out string table */
    mk_stringhandles(dde_inst,str);
/* Init TOPIC/ITEM array */
    server_fill(logintopics,str+1);
/* Set exec command */
    server_setexec(docmd);
/* Start server */
    server(str[0].hsz,logintopics);
/* Open dialog box */
    main=MakeProcInstance(main_dlg,hInst);
    DialogBox(hInst,MAIN_DLG,NULL,main);
/* Done -- free everything */
    FreeProcInstance(main);
    server_end();
```

```
      free_stringhandles(dde_inst,str);
      server_done();
      return FALSE;
      }



/* Find data from INI file */
HDDEDATA do_user(HSZ hsz1,HSZ hszitem)
  {
  char item[66],result[66],user[66];
  DdeQueryString(dde_inst,hszitem,item,sizeof(item),
               CP_WINANSI);
  SendDlgItemMessage(dialog,USERS,LB_GETTEXT,
       SendDlgItemMessage(dialog,USERS,LB_GETCURSEL,0,0),
                        (DWORD)user);
  GetPrivateProfileString(user,item,"N/A",result,
                        sizeof(result),"LOGIN.INI");
  return DdeCreateDataHandle(dde_inst,result,
                        strlen(result)+1,0,hszitem,
                        CF_TEXT,0);
  }
```

6

OLE Overview

WHAT'S IN THIS CHAPTER

This chapter lays the groundwork for writing OLE 2.0 clients and servers. You'll learn to use both the registration database and the OLE 2.0 structured storage system. Many important OLE terms are defined.

PREREQUISITES

Understanding of Windows programming. Familiarity with OLE 2.0 from the user's perspective. You should have the OLE 2.01 SDK.

As powerful as DDE is, there are some inherent problems with it. DDE clients can handle only data they understand. For example, if your DDE client knows only how to import bitmaps, the user cannot create a link to a wave file. Worse, if you extend your client program to accept wave files, you have to write all of the code needed to manipulate wave files.

OLE allows server programs to manage data inside other applications. The server is responsible for creating and editing the data. It must provide a display representation of the data or draw the data itself. For example, a program can use an OLE server for wave files to place an audio clip into a document. The OLE server can provide a bitmap of a loudspeaker for display purposes. When the user double-clicks the bitmap, the OLE server plays the wave file. You can write OLE programs that receive data from a server, but that is an unusual case.

OLE 1.0 deals strictly with creating compound documents. OLE 2.0, however, is more than just an IPC protocol; it provides an object-oriented API. You can access many traditional Windows API calls via object interfaces and extend the API with your own objects. For example, OLE 2.0 supplies a powerful interface to the file system that allows transaction processing, long file names, and other important enhancements. You may want to use OLE in your program just for these superior new features.

Currently, the OLE API is an object-oriented layer built on top of the traditional API. Soon, the traditional API will be a compatibility layer on top of the object-oriented API. Using the OLE object-oriented layer will have a very slight performance penalty today, but in the future it will be the method of choice.

OLE Myths

OLE has an undeserved reputation for being difficult. If you approach OLE methodically and in carefully planned steps, you won't have any problems. Here are some common OLE misconceptions:

- **MYTH #1:** OLE programs require C++.
  While OLE uses objects, there is nothing to keep you from writing OLE programs in C or any other language that you can use to write a regular Windows program. If you use C++, the compiler will do some initialization for you, but it isn't difficult to do in C either.

- **MYTH #2:** OLE requires you to change your file format.
  OLE does not require you to change your existing file format. Once you learn about OLE's advanced file system (the IStorage structured storage interface), you will probably want to change your file format to use it. You can still support your old format at the same time, if you like. However, it's fine not to change your file format. OLE allows you to store objects in an OLE structured file, a database, a memory region, or even your old file format.

- **MYTH #3:** OLE programs need many complex dialogs.
  This myth is not completely false; your programs will need several complex dialogs to support OLE, but you no longer need to write them yourself. Starting with OLE 2.0, Microsoft provides sample OLE dialogs that you can use instead of rolling your own. The dialogs compile to a DLL, and Microsoft provides the source code in case you want to customize them.

- **MYTH #4:** OLE 2.0 programs are harder to write than OLE 1.0 programs.

  In reality, OLE 2.0 provides functionality that you needed to write yourself under OLE 1.0. You can still place OLE 1.0 objects in an OLE 2.0 document, and you can put OLE 2.0 objects in an OLE 1.0 document.

Definitions

OLE's documentation uses some familiar words in unfamiliar ways. If you want to read the OLE documentation, you need to keep the meaning of these words clearly fixed in your mind.

Client/Container

Programs that can incorporate OLE data are OLE **clients**. A client simply displays data and accepts commands destined for the data. Most new OLE documentation calls clients **containers** since they contain objects.

Server/Object Application

An OLE **server** creates OLE data and performs operations on it. Users (via clients) request these operations (like EDIT or RUN, for example). Newer OLE documentation refers to servers as **object applications**.

Objects

OLE treats its data as **objects**. This is consistent with OLE's basic philosophy—OLE data is a hidden package, and its contents are not necessarily known by the application using it. Each object retains an association with its server application, and this application is responsible for servicing (that is, drawing, running, editing, and so on) the object.

Note that these objects are not the same as C++ objects, although you can create them in C++ if you like.

Linked Object

There are two ways to insert an OLE object into a document. Your first choice is to create a **link**, which inserts a reference to an OLE object into the document. The OLE object resides in a separate file; several clients can share a single linked object. For example, you might link a cell in a spreadsheet file into several word processor documents. Many clients and servers do not support linking (see miniserver below).

Embedded Object

The most common way to insert an object is via **embedding**. A client application owns and stores each embedded object it contains. The server still processes the object, but the client provides storage for it, usually inside its existing document file.

Miniserver

Some OLE servers cannot save files—they only support embedded objects. These servers are **miniservers**. Programs like MSDRAW and WORDART that come with Microsoft Word are examples of miniservers.

Verbs

Servers can accept commands, or **verbs**, to apply to objects. The most common verb is EDIT, but a server can support any number of verbs. A sound object, for example, might support both EDIT and PLAY verbs.

Compound Document

A document that contains linked or embedded objects is a **compound document**. With OLE 2.0, the OLE system provides optional services to simplify saving compound documents to disk.

Registration

Windows provides a **registration database** that is available to all programs. It ordinarily contains information about file associations and OLE applications.

The REGEDIT program allows users to examine and modify the database. (Windows does not install REGEDIT in Program Manager by default, but the file REGEDIT.EXE is in your Windows directory.) For programmers, the /v (verbose) option is usually useful (see Figure 6-1).

The registration database contains keys that identify attributes and may have an associated value and subkeys. The registra-

Figure 6-1. The Registration Editor

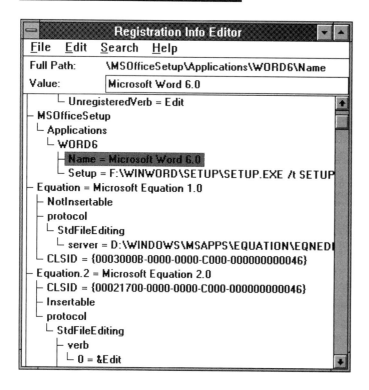

tion database arranges keys and subkeys in a directory-like hierarchy. For example, here is a typical entry in the database:

```
\.hlp\shell\open\command=winhelp.exe %1
```

This composite key has three individual keys (.hlp, shell, and open). Each key is separated by a backslash (just like directories). The value of the command item is the string "winhelp.exe %1".

For OLE, the registration database stores information about available objects and the servers that supply them. This prevents the dilemma that DDE programs face when they can't find a running server. A DDE client has to guess at the server program's name, but an OLE client can look up a server's program name.

Interface

An **interface** is simply a table of function pointers that perform operations on an object. This is the only part of an OLE object its users ever see. Many programmers call this table a V-Table (or VTBL). The table follows the C++ convention for virtual function tables.

For example, suppose you ask the OLE libraries for a structured storage object. Instead of sending you the entire object, it returns a pointer to the object's interface table. Each entry in the table performs some predefined operation. Of course, the object and its user must agree what those operations are, what arguments the calls take, and their return value. Where that function pointer goes or how it does its work is not important to the object user.

Older OLE documentation may call an interface a **protocol** (protocols and interfaces are the synonymous).

Using the Registration Database

The registration database has a simple API (see Table 6-1). You need to include SHELLAPI.H with programs that use the database. Before you can work with the database, you must open a key using RegOpenKey(); you can open the root key by specifying HKEY_CLASSES_ROOT. This returns a key handle of type HKEY.

Table 6-1. Registration API

Function	Description
RegCreateKey	Creates or opens a key handle
RegOpenKey	Opens an existing key
RegDeleteKey	Deletes a subkey of an open key
RegQueryValue	Reads the value of an open key (or a subkey)
RegSetValue	Sets the value of an open key or subkey
RegEnumKey	Enumerates subkeys of an open key
RegCloseKey	Closes a key handle

Once you have an open key, you can enumerate its subkeys, retrieve or modify its value, create a new subkey, and so on. You can also work with any of its subkeys without opening them. Use RegCloseKey() to release the open key.

Listing 6-1 shows REGLIST, a simple program that enumerates all of the top level keys in your registration database. For simplicity, it uses the WPRINT library, which is on the companion disk.

The RegEnumKey() function takes four parameters: the handle of the open key, a subkey number (zero-based), a buffer for the key name, and the length of the buffer. To work down the list of keys, set the subkey number to zero on the first call and increment it for each subsequent call. The function returns an error when there are no more subkeys.

You won't make much use of the registration database until you write an object application (server). Although OLE 2.0 isolates you from the database more than OLE 1.0 did you will still need to work with the database sometimes.

Listing 6-1. REGLIST.C

```
/* REGEDIT Example program -- uses WPRINT library to print
   Registration database entries */
#include <windows.h>
#include <shellapi.h>
#include "wprint.h"


/* WPRINT requires this global to be set */
HANDLE hInst;


/* Main window function */
int PASCAL WinMain(HANDLE hInstance, HANDLE prev,
                LPSTR cmdline, int show)
  {
  HKEY root;
  char name[1024];
  DWORD i;
  hInst=hInstance;
/* Open root key */
  if (RegOpenKey(HKEY_CLASSES_ROOT,NULL,&root)==ERROR_SUCCESS)
    {
/* scan keys */
    for (i=0;
        RegEnumKey(root,i,name,sizeof(name))==ERROR_SUCCESS;
        i++)
```

```
    {
    win_printf("Registration Database Entry","%s",name);
    }
  }
/* close down */
  RegCloseKey(root);
  return FALSE;
  }
```

OLE Structured Storage

A key OLE 2.0 technology is the structured storage system (SSS). Although it primarily supports compound document storage, you may find you want to use it for all of your file storage needs.

SSS essentially converts a single MSDOS file into a complete file system. The file can contain storages (analogous to directories) and streams (files). Storages can contain other storages, just as directories can hold subdirectories.

The OLE SSS provides the usual operations for streams that you expect for files (open, close, read, write, and seek). It also supplies functions for transaction processing. Thus, you can make changes to a file that won't become permanent until you commit the file. You can undo your changes by performing a rollback. Unlike MSDOS, SSS allows long stream and storage names, stores creation and access times, and provides a variety of sharing and protection methods.

Don't worry about how to use the SSS right now. The example later in this chapter uses it to store multiple C source files in one SSS storage and later unpack them into the original files.

Using OLE Interfaces

The key to using OLE is understanding interfaces. You can segregate OLE functions into two broad classes: API functions and interface functions. API functions such as StgOpen-Storage() are just like ordinary Windows functions. You will find them listed in the OLE 2.0 SDK reference in a format similar to that of the ordinary SDK documentation.

Interface functions are another matter. They are analogous to C++ member functions, and the SDK documentation assumes you are using C++. Therefore, the documentation shows these functions like this:

```
HRESULT IStorage::CreateStream(...)
```

All this means is that there is a function pointer in all IStorage interfaces that will invoke the CreateStream function. With C++, this is very natural. If variable p is a pointer to an IStorage interface, you just say this:

```
p->CreateStream(...);
```

However, from C things are more complex. You have to perform one additional dereference and duplicate C++'s this pointer (C++ always passes an object pointer as a hidden first parameter to member function calls; don't worry about why). From C, the call looks like this:

```
p->lpVtbl->CreateStream(p,...);
```

By using the preprocessor, you can reduce the complexity of these OLE calls. The file C_OLE.H on the companion disk allows you to make simplified calls from either C or C++. You

will learn more about C_OLE.H when you examine the
sample program later in this chapter.

By now, all of this should seem very unclear. Don't worry—
explaining interfaces is harder than using them. A quick look
at some code will clear up everything.

Listing 6-2. ARCHIVE.C

```
/* C file archive program -- uses OLE structured storage */
#include <windows.h>
#include <ole2.h>
#include <stdio.h>
#include <dos.h>
#include <fcntl.h>
#include <ctype.h>
#include "c_ole.h"


HANDLE hInst;


CATCHBUF xitbuf;


/* General error */
error(HRESULT err,int n)
  {
  char msg[64];
  wsprintf(msg,"Error %d (%lx)\n",n,err);
  MessageBox(NULL,msg,NULL,MB_OK|MB_ICONSTOP);
  Throw(xitbuf,1);
  }


#define errorck(a,b) if (a!=S_OK) error(a,b)


/* Unarchive storage */
```

```
void unarchive(LPSTORAGE sto,LPSTREAM list)
  {
  unsigned long cb;
  int rv,i;
  HFILE fh;
  HRESULT rc;
  char buf[2048];
  LPSTREAM ifile;
/* Read file name until NULL terminator */
  while (1)
    {
    i=0;
    do
      {
      Read(list,buf+i,1,&cb);
      if (!cb) return;
      } while (buf[i++]);
    fh=_lcreat(buf,0);
    if (!fh) error(0,7);
/* Open stream */
    OpenStream(sto,buf,NULL,
        STGM_READ|STGM_SHARE_EXCLUSIVE|STGM_DIRECT,0,&ifile);
/* Copy file out */
    do
      {
      rc=Read(ifile,buf,sizeof(buf),&cb);
      if (rc==S_OK) _lwrite(fh,buf,(UINT)cb);
      } while (rc==S_OK&&cb);
    _lclose(fh);
    Release(ifile);
    }
  }
/* Create archive */
```

```
void archive(LPSTORAGE sto,LPSTREAM list)
  {
  struct find_t ff;
  int rv;
  unsigned long cb;
  HRESULT rc;
  char buf[2048];
  HFILE fh;
/* Search for files */
  rv=_dos_findfirst("*.c",0,&ff);
  while (!rv)
    {
    int ln;
    LPSTREAM data;
/* Open file */
    fh=_lopen(ff.name,READ);
    if (fh)
      {
/* Open stream for file */
      rc=CreateStream(sto,ff.name,
                      STGM_READWRITE|STGM_SHARE_EXCLUSIVE|
                      STGM_DIRECT|STGM_CREATE,NULL,NULL,&data);
      errorck(rc,3);
/* Read block */
      while ((ln=_lread(fh,buf,sizeof(buf)))>0)
        {
/* Write to storage */
        rc=Write(data,buf,ln,&cb);
        errorck(rc,4);
        }
      _lclose(fh);
      Release(data);
/* Write name to file list */
```

```
      rc=Write(list,ff.name,strlen(ff.name)+1,&cb);
      errorck(rc,5);
      }

   rv=_dos_findnext(&ff);
   }
 }


/* Main window function */
int PASCAL WinMain(HANDLE hInstance, HANDLE prev,
              LPSTR cmdline, int show)
 {
 DWORD ver;
 hInst = hInstance;
 ver=CoBuildVersion();
 if (HIWORD(ver)<20)
   {
   MessageBox(NULL,
              "This program requires OLE Version 2.x",
              NULL,MB_OK|MB_ICONSTOP);
   return 1;
   }
 if (Catch(xitbuf))
   {
   CoUninitialize();
   return 0;
   }
 if (CoInitialize(NULL)==S_OK)
   {
   LPSTORAGE main_sto;
   LPSTREAM filelist;
   HRESULT rc;
```

```
    if (*cmdline=='-')
      {
      do cmdline++; while (isspace(*cmdline));
/* open file for unarchive */
      rc=StgOpenStorage(cmdline,NULL,
                        STGM_READ|STGM_SHARE_EXCLUSIVE|
                         STGM_DIRECT,
                        NULL,0,&main_sto);
      errorck(rc,1);
/* Open file list */
      rc=OpenStream(main_sto,
                    ".flist",NULL,
                    STGM_READ|STGM_SHARE_EXCLUSIVE|STGM_DIRECT,
                    0,&filelist);
      errorck(rc,2);
      unarchive(main_sto,filelist);
      MessageBox(NULL,"Unarchive Done","Notice",MB_OK);
      return FALSE;
      }


    if (*cmdline=='+')
        do cmdline++; while (isspace(*cmdline));
/* Make new archive */
    rc=StgCreateDocfile(cmdline,
                        STGM_CREATE|STGM_READWRITE|
                        STGM_SHARE_EXCLUSIVE|STGM_DIRECT,
                        0,&main_sto);
    errorck(rc,1);
/* Make file list */
    rc=CreateStream(main_sto,".flist",
                        STGM_READWRITE|STGM_SHARE_EXCLUSIVE|
                        STGM_DIRECT|STGM_CREATE,NULL,NULL,
                        &filelist);
```

```
    errorck(rc,2);
    archive(main_sto,filelist);
    Release(filelist);
    Release(main_sto);
    CoUninitialize();
    MessageBox(NULL,"Archive Done","Notice",MB_OK);
    }
  return FALSE;
  }
```

Listing 6-2 shows ARCHIVE.C, a simple program that uses OLE's structured storage to store multiple C source files in a single DOS file. If you specify a file name preceded by a + character, ARCHIVE creates an archive with that name that contains all the .C files in the current directory. If you precede the file name with a – character, ARCHIVE restores the files from the archive in the current directory. Let's look at the important parts of ARCHIVE, starting with WinMain(). You'll find a list of functions ARCHIVE uses in Table 6-2.

Table 6-2. OLE Functions used by ARCHIVE

Function	Description
CoBuildVersion	Finds version of OLE libraries
CoInitialize	Sets up component object portion of OLE
CoUninitialize	Shuts down component object portion of OLE
StgCreateDocfile	Creates a new storage
StgOpenStorage	Opens an existing storage
CreateStream	Creates a stream in a storage
OpenStream	Opens an existing stream
Write	Writes to a stream
Read	Reads from a stream
Release	Release an object

Initialization

The first thing most OLE programs need to check is the OLE version. The CoBuildVersion() API function returns a version number that you can check. Next, ARCHIVE calls CoInitialize(). If the application used OLE documents, it would call OleInitialize() instead of CoInitialize(). However, since this program does not deal with documents, CoInitialize() is the correct call.

If CoInitialize() returns success, then you must call CoUninitialize() before your program terminates. However, don't call CoUninitialize() if the CoInitialize() call fails.

Getting an Interface Pointer

There are several possible methods for getting an interface pointer, but many of them assume you already have one interface pointer. For a program like ARCHIVE, you must call an ordinary API that returns an interface pointer. The StgOpenStorage() and StgCreateDocfile() calls do just that. They take an operating system file name (passed in via the cmdline parameter here) and convert it to an OLE structured storage object.

In the case of archive creation (the + option), StgCreateDocfile() makes a new storage object and places its interface pointer in the main_sto variable. After that, there is a call to CreateStream(). This makes a new stream in the storage object named .flist. This stream stores a list of files that the archive contains.

Calling Interface Functions From C

If you look in the OLE 2.0 reference for a function named CreateStream(), you won't find it, but you will find an IStorage member function named CreateStream().

To call this function from C, you must use the lpVtbl field of the interface pointer. Also, you must always pass the interface pointer as the first argument to the function. Since C++ does this automatically, the API documentation omits this argument. A C call looks like this:

```
ip->lpVtbl->CreateStream(ip,....);
```

Using the preprocessor, we can simplify calling these C++ member functions from C. In C_OLE.H on the companion disk, you'll find this define:

```
#define CreateStream(a,b,c,d,e,f) \
    a->lpVtbl->CreateStream(a,b,c,d,e,f)
```

This makes your C code more readable and prevents you from forgetting to pass the object as the first parameter. If you switch between C++ and C, C_OLE.H provides another define to keep your code consistent:

```
#define CreateStream(a,b,c,d,e,f) \
    a->CreateStream(b,c,d,e,f)
```

C_OLE.H provides many common defines for OLE functions and automatically adjusts for C or C++. You can easily add any other functions you need to this file. If you use only C++, these defines have little value.

Now you can look up IStorage::CreateStream() in the API reference and see what it does. ARCHIVE uses the C_OLE.H defines for IStorage::CreateStream(), IStream::Write(), IStream::Read(), IUnknown::Release(), and IStorage::OpenStream().

IUnknown

Look carefully at the last list of functions. There is a function for the IUnknown interface, yet ARCHIVE doesn't have any objects of type IUnknown, does it? In truth, nearly all OLE objects can be of type IUnknown in addition to their regular class (that's polymorphism, if you're an object-oriented programmer).

Remember that each interface pointer refers to a table of function pointers. The first three slots of each table supports the IUnknown interface (see Table 6-3). Therefore, you can always treat an object as IUnknown. The IUnknown::Query-Interface() function allows you to learn about other interfaces an object supports.

Table 6-3. IUnknown interface

Function	Description
QueryInterface	Finds other interfaces an object supports
AddRef	Increments object's reference counter
Release	Decrement object's reference counter (free object when counter is zero)

Reference Counting

The other two functions in the IUnknown interface are IUnknown::AddRef() and IUnknown::Release(), both of which control the allocation of resources for objects. Each object stores its own reference count. For example, in ARCHIVE the call to StgCreateDocfile() returns an IStorage interface pointer. Before it returns, StgCreateDocfile() calls the new object's AddRef() function. This increments the object's reference count to one. Later, when ARCHIVE is done with the object, it calls the Release function:

```
Release(main_obj);
```

or

```
main_obj->lpVtbl->Release(main_obj);
```

This decrements the object's reference count. When the reference count is zero, the object destroys itself.

If you go by the book, you should call AddRef() on an object every time you make a copy of its pointer. However, in practice you can often avoid this. For example, when ARCHIVE passes main_sto and filelist to the archive() function, there is no need to update the reference count. The original object's lifetime is longer than the copy, so you can safely ignore the copy. However, if there is any chance that you will call Release() on the original pointer before you are through with the copies, you must call AddRef() and Release() for the subroutine's copy.

There are three common cases when you must use AddRef() and Release() on your pointers:

• If you use an interface pointer in a global variable, you must manage its reference count. You can't be sure another routine won't release the global pointer before you are done.

• Any interface pointer you return must AddRef() the pointer. For example, when you write an IUnknown::QueryInterface() function, it must call AddRef() on the returned pointer.

• You must call AddRef() on any pointer that you pass to another function as an in/out parameter. The function will call Release() on the pointer, and then put another pointer in its place. The subroutine will call AddRef() on that pointer.

It is important to realize that one object may support many interfaces. When this is the case, one reference count serves the entire object, no matter what interface you use to call AddRef() and Release(). It doesn't matter if anyone is using a specific interface—it matters that the object is in use.

HRESULTs and SCODEs

OLE functions return error codes as an HRESULT (see Figure 6-2). If the function succeeds, the HRESULT is usually zero (the S_OK or NOERROR constants). If the function wants to return more information, it can use the fields of the HRESULT to specify more information about its success or failure (depending on bit 31 of the HRESULT).

Figure 6-2. HRESULT

S	Context	Facility	Code

S - Severity (1=error, 0=success)
Context - 0 for SCODE, handle for HRESULT
Facility - Which subsystem; 0=general, 3=STORAGE, etc. (see SCODE.H)
Code - Failure or success code

An SCODE is what you get when you remove the context field from an HRESULT. You can use the GetSCode() macro to convert an HRESULT to an SCODE.

The important part of an SCODE or HRESULT is the CODE field. This number corresponds to the error numbers you will find in the OLE header files. For example, in STORAGE.H you will find the following define:

```
#define STG_E_FILENOTFOUND \
  MAKE_SCODE(SEVERITY_ERROR,FACILITY_STORAGE,0x02)
```

The 0x02 is the number that appears in the code field when the storage system reports that it can't find a file.

More About ARCHIVE

ARCHIVE uses a separate storage stream for each file and a special stream (.flist) to store the names of the files in the storage. A better approach is to use an OLE enumerator. An enumerator is an object that supports functions to enumerate over a list. However, to keep things simple, ARCHIVE just stores the names in a separate stream.

The archive() function creates new archives. To locate and read the files, archive() uses ordinary file I/O calls. For each file, it creates a stream in the main storage and writes the file's data to it. When ARCHIVE finishes with a file, it closes the file, calls Release() for the stream, and writes the file name to the .flist stream.

Unarchiving is essentially the reverse process. The .flist stream provides file names that the unarchive() function creates using _lcreat(), a standard Windows function. For each file name, unarchive() opens the stream and copies its data to the file. When the operation is complete, unarchive() closes the file and call Release() on the stream.

ARCHIVE doesn't attempt to do any compression, and the SSS has a good deal of overhead. Unless you archive many small files, you probably won't save disk space by using ARCHIVE. Still, ARCHIVE shows off many of the fine points of using the SSS and OLE interfaces.

Compiling ARCHIVE

You can compile ARCHIVE just as you do any other Windows application (see the makefiles on the companion disk). Be sure to add the \OLE2\INCLUDE directory in your include and library paths. You must also include the OLE2.LIB and STORAGE.LIB libraries when linking. If you are using an ordinary ANSI C compiler, you probably will need the NONAMELESSUNION define as well. All of the examples in this book assume the NONAMELESSUNION define.

Using an Enumerator

Version 1.1 of ARCHIVE (see the excerpt of ARCHIVE1.C in Listing 6-3) uses an enumerator instead of the .flist stream to find the names of its files. The .flist stream is still present, but it contains only the string ARCHIVE.1.

Listing 6-3. Excerpts from ARCHIVE1.C

```
/* Unarchive storage */
void unarchive(LPSTORAGE sto,LPSTREAM list)
  {
  unsigned long cb;
  int rv,i;
  HFILE fh;
  HRESULT rc;
  char buf[2048],*bp;
  LPSTREAM ifile;
  LPENUMSTATSTG dir;
  STATSTG stat;
  LPMALLOC pmalloc;
  CoGetMalloc(MEMCTX_TASK,&pmalloc);
/* Enumerate files */
```

```
    EnumElements(sto,0,NULL,0,&dir);
    while (Next(dir,1,&stat,NULL)==S_OK)
      {
      bp=buf;
      while (*bp++=*stat.pwcsName++);   /* make local copy */
/* Free returned pointer */
      Free(pmalloc,stat.pwcsName);
      if (*buf=='.') continue;    /* skip .flist */
      fh=_lcreat(buf,0);
      if (fh==-1) error(0,7);
/* Open stream */
      OpenStream(sto,buf,NULL,STGM_READ|STGM_SHARE_EXCLUSIVE|
                          STGM_DIRECT,0,&ifile);
/* Copy file out */
      do
        {
        rc=Read(ifile,buf,sizeof(buf),&cb);
        if (rc==S_OK) _lwrite(fh,buf,(UINT)cb);
        } while (rc==S_OK&&cb);
      _lclose(fh);
      Release(ifile);
      }
    Release(dir);
    Release(pmalloc);
    }
```

The unarchive() function is where most of the changes
for enumeration reside. First, ARCHIVE1 needs an
LPENUMSTATSTG variable to hold the enumerator (the dir
variable). This enumerator returns a sequence of STATSTG
structures. The structures contain the element name and other
data about the current stream or substorage.

The IStorage::EnumElements() call creates the enumerator for the archive's main storage. Each call to IEnumStatStg::Next() returns a STATSTG structure. Since the name in the structure is a far pointer, ARCHIVE1 copies it to a local buffer.

This is simple enough, except for one slight hitch. The enumerator uses OLE's IMalloc interface to dynamically allocate the memory that holds the file name in the STATSTG structure. ARCHIVE1 is responsible for freeing the memory.

Before ARCHIVE1 can free the memory, it needs a pointer to an IMalloc interface. The CoGetMalloc() call near the top of the unarchive() function finds this pointer (pmalloc). unarchive() must now call IMalloc::Free() each time it is finished with a file name. When all processing is complete, unarchive() must call Release() for the enumerator and the IMalloc interface.

Enumerators are common in OLE. All enumerators share a common set of method functions (see Table 6-4) but return different items.

Table 6-4. Enumerator interface

Function	Description
Next	Returns next items in enumeration
Skip	Skips items in enumeration
Reset	Starts enumeration again
Clone	Copies enumerator with same state

Summary

Although OLE is a bit different from traditional Windows programming, you'll find it easy to learn and use once you get started. It seems that future versions of Windows will continue this object-oriented approach, so you might as well bite the bullet and start now.

In this chapter (and in this book), you will see OLE code written in C. This allows C and C++ programmers alike to follow the examples and explanations. However, you should consider switching to C++ if you haven't already. Along with its other advantages, C++ simplifies OLE programming. Using C++ also allows you to use advanced class libraries such as Microsoft's Foundation Classes (MFC) and Borland's Object Windows Library (OWL).

Still, if you have too much code to convert (or if you are simply stubborn), you can still participate in the OLE revolution—despite what you may have heard. OLE is purposely language-independent, and you can write for OLE in C with little difficulty.

7

OLE Containers

WHAT'S IN THIS CHAPTER

In this chapter, you'll study the implementation of a basic OLE container application.

PREREQUISITES

Understanding of the concepts in Chapter 6. You should have the OLE 2.01 SDK documentation.

Writing an OLE 2.0 container application need not be difficult. The key is to ignore all the advanced OLE 2.0 features that you don't need (or at least wait until you need them to learn about them).

The best way to understand OLE is to read source code. This chapter's example program, CONTAIN, is presented in several parts. Each part builds on the previous parts until it becomes a fairly complete OLE client, or container.

About CONTAIN

CONTAIN is a simple OLE client that provides a place to put OLE objects. You can perform elementary operations, such as delete, move, and resize on the objects.

Of course, your programs will need to do more. Still, you shouldn't have to wade through application-specific code while wrestling with OLE. Once you understand CONTAIN, you should have no problem adding OLE to your applications.

In that spirit, CONTAIN often takes some shortcuts that don't apply directly to OLE. For example, to resize an object, you select it and drag with the right mouse key. This isn't the usual user interface for resizing objects, but if you understand how to resize an object, you can work out the interface to match your existing code.

OLE is very flexible and will allow your program to do as much work as you want it to do. CONTAIN lets the OLE libraries do as much work as possible. CONTAIN also uses the OLE2UI library that Microsoft ships with the OLE 2.0 SDK (see the box entitled "About OLE2UI"). Using this library can shave weeks off your application development time.

About OLE2UI

Microsoft includes the OLE2UI library with the OLE 2.01 SDK (you can find it in the SAMP\OLE2UI directory). This library contains many useful functions that you can call from inside your code. Many developers will want to modify the OLE2UI dialogs (to support other languages, for example). Therefore, Microsoft supplies the source code to OLE2UI—you must build the library yourself.

To use OLE2UI with your application, you should recompile it using the supplied makefiles (see the Appendix for more information about compiling OLE2UI with Borland C). You can link it with your program as an ordinary library, or you can create a DLL. To avoid compatibility problems, don't name the DLL OLE2UI. Each developer should assign a unique name to the DLL.

Since CONTAIN doesn't modify OLE2UI, it can use the OUTLUI.DLL that Microsoft's OUTLINE sample uses. However, since Microsoft does not permit you to redistribute OUTLUI.DLL, CONTAIN uses its own version of the OLE2UI library, AWOLEUI.DLL. This DLL uses Borland C, but otherwise it's functionally the same as OUTLUI.DLL. Since Borland C does not allow very long indentifiers, the OleStdGetObjectDescriptorDataFrom-OleObject() function is truncated to OleStdGetObjectDescriptorDataFro() in this DLL (see the Appendix for ways to set your .DEF file to circumvent this problem).

Since CONTAIN will progress through several generations, its source code is in separate directories on the disk. CONTAIN1 is the first generation of CONTAIN, CONTAIN2 is the next, and so on. As the following list indicates, each version of CONTAIN adds new features:

- CONTAIN1—A basic windows program that uses structured storage, but does not support embedding

- CONTAIN2—Allows you to insert objects via the Insert Object menu

- CONTAIN3—Allows you to use verbs on objects in the document

- CONTAIN4—Embeds objects from the clipboard

- CONTAIN5—Supports linking from any server that supports it

- CONTAIN6—Adds "Paste Special" support

- CONTAIN7—Allows you to drag and drop between documents, within a document, or between other OLE drag and drop applications (See the box entitled "About the Versions of CONTAIN" for more information.) '

CONTAIN1—The Beginning

Often, you will add OLE 2.0 to an existing application. Even if you are starting from scratch, you should get your application working without OLE before trying to add it. Of course, you need to plan ahead for OLE, if possible. Just try to get one thing working at a time. When your application is functional, you can add OLE support at that time.

CONTAIN1 is not the most sophisticated application you will ever see. It has a simple menu bar and a client area. It can load and save files (using the OLE storage system), but they don't contain anything. This is the base CONTAIN application. Since CONTAIN works only with OLE, building it without OLE support is boring. However, this is a good time to look at CONTAIN's basic document structure.

About the Versions of CONTAIN

Like most real applications, CONTAIN didn't start out as an OLE client. It also didn't become a full OLE client in one step. Therefore, the companion disk has subdirectories for each version of CONTAIN. The early versions of CONTAIN (CONTAIN1-CONTAIN5) may be rough around the edges; CONTAIN6 is the final, working version, and CONTAIN7 adds drag-and-drop support. Still, it is valuable to examine the code through each stage of its evolution.

Even if you are writing a new application, you should get your base functions working before proceeding to OLE. The advantage you have when starting from scratch is the freedom to design OLE in from the beginning.

CONTAIN maintains a linked list of DOCOBJECT structures. Each structure represents one OLE item (later, these will be client sites). Each DOCOBJECT structure contains the following items:

bound   A rectangle that describes the object's position

next   A pointer to the next structure (or NULL at the end of the list)

prev   A pointer to the previous structure (or NULL at the beginning of the list)

DOCOBJECT grows larger as CONTAIN gets more OLE support. The address of the first item in the list is in the dochead variable.

CONTAIN also has a doc_info structure that contains a magic number to identify CONTAIN files and the size of the document's window. This structure will have more fields later, too.

CONTAIN relies on many global variables (like dochead and doc_info). Some other global variables are

topwindow	The main window handle
dragging	Flag indicates that user is dragging (moving) an object
resize	Flag indicates that user is resizing an object
dragx,dragy	Current drag or resize position
filename	Current filename
main_sto	Main OLE storage (see Chapter 6)
dirty	File needs saving

At this point, CONTAIN is just an ordinary Windows program. The update() routine handles WM_PAINT messages by walking the linked list and drawing what it finds. At this point, it doesn't know how to draw anything; since the list is always empty, this doesn't matter.

The menu() function vectors the File menu selections to the proper routines. Again, these functions can't really save and load objects, but there are no objects in the document anyway.

CONTAIN2—The Next Generation

To start adding OLE client capability to CONTAIN, you need to understand OLE compound documents. At a minimum, an OLE client application must:

- Supply the IClientSite and IAdviseSink interfaces for each OLE object it contains. The IClientSite interface manages the object. The IAdviseSink interface receives notifications concerning the object from the server.

- Provide an OLE storage for each object it contains.

- Manage the creation and destruction of objects.

- Draw the objects as part of its WM_PAINT handler.

- Save and load objects from a file or storage.

Luckily, OLE and OLE2UI do much of this work or reduce it to a few lines of simple code.

Providing an interface is just a fancy way of saying that your program must supply certain routines and keep an array of function pointers to pass to certain OLE API calls. By creating these interfaces, you are providing an OLE object. Each embedded or linked object in your document resides in some data structure you define (the DOCOBJECT list in CONTAIN, for example). The IClientSite and IAdviseSink interfaces simply give the outside world access to your private data. Since the interface is simply a list of function pointers, you are free to store your data any way that you like.

OLE provides several macros to help you define interfaces and interface functions (see the box entitled "The STDMETHOD Macros" for more details).

The OLE2UI library provides all the special dialogs you need in the same way that the common dialog library provides file open dialogs. It also creates new OLE objects for you as a result of user interaction with these dialogs. Unless you are a masochist, use these dialogs. They are flexible, and you can optionally use custom dialog templates to modify their appearance.

The STDMETHOD Macros

The OLE toolkit provides several macros to assist you in declaring and implementing interfaces. When you write interface functions, you can use the STDMETHODIMP and STDMETHODIMP_ macros. These macros expand like this:

```
STDMETHODIMP foo()
        .
        .
        .
STDMETHODIMP_(BOOL) bar()
```

expands to:

```
HRESULT __export FAR CDECL foo()
        .
        .
        .
BOOL __export FAR CDECL bar()
```

As you port code to other platforms, these macros may expand to other values, so it is worthwhile to use the macros. For example, the OLE2 headers have alternate values for the Macintosh platform.

Other macros can assist in defining interfaces in header files such that C and C++ code can use the same declarations. Here is a typical (but imaginary) interface definition using those macros:

```
#undef INTERFACE
#define INTERFACE IUFPObj

DECLARE_INTERFACE_(IUFPObj,IUnknown)
  {
  STDMETHOD(QueryInterface)(THIS_ REFIID riid,
           LPVOID FAR *ppvObj) PURE;
  STDMETHOD_(ULONG,AddRef)(THIS) PURE;
  STDMETHOD_(ULONG,Release)(THIS) PURE;
  STDMETHOD(Council)(THIS) PURE;
  };
```

The preceding code expands to appropriate definitions for C or C++. The STDMETHOD macro assumes the function returns an HRESULT. The STDMETHOD_ macro allows you to override the return type. For C++, the THIS and THIS_ macros expand to empty strings. Under C, they generate *INTERFACE FAR* This* and *INTERFACE FAR* This,*, respectively. Similarly, the PURE macro expands to nothing for a C program, and the =0 string for C++.

CONTAIN doesn't use the declaration macros, although it could. However, the interface functions in CON_IF.C make extensive use of the STDMETHODIMP and STDMETHODIMP_ macros.

OLE2UI does most of the work when creating an object. Still, your program has the following responsibilities:

- Integrate some information about the object into your document

- Provide an open storage for the object

- Tell the object your application's name and how you want it to display

Drawing an OLE object is simple. The OLE library has two calls you can use to draw an object of a certain size on a device context (OleDraw() and the IViewObject::Draw() function). You may have to do some work to map coordinates unless your application uses MM_HIMETRIC already. All OLE functions use the MM_HIMETRIC mapping mode and expect object coordinates to be in that mode.

CONTAIN2's New Data

Here is CONTAIN's new document data structure:

```
typedef struct doc_object
  {
  char objname[13];
  DWORD refct;
  RECT bound;
  struct doc_object *prev,*next;
  LPOLEOBJECT ole_obj;
  LPSTORAGE obj_sto;
  unsigned int flags;
  struct _cs_interface
    {
    IOleClientSiteVtbl FAR *lpVtbl;
    struct doc_object *object;
    } cs_interface;
  struct _as_interface
    {
    IAdviseSinkVtbl FAR *lpVtbl;
    struct doc_object *object;
    } as_interface;
  DWORD dtype;       /* OleDraw aspect */
  } DOCOBJECT;
```

The objname field stores an arbitrary and unique string that refers to the object. This simply distinguishes the object from other objects in the document. CONTAIN uses the string OBJxxxxxxxx, where xxxxxxxx is a zero-filled 32-bit hex number.

Remember that CONTAIN has to provide two interfaces for each OLE object it contains. Since all interfaces contain the IUnknown interface, CONTAIN has to maintain a reference count to support the AddRef() and Release() functions (see Chapter 6 for more about IUnknown). The refct field provides this reference count. When the count reaches zero, CONTAIN can free the object.

The ole_obj and ole_sto fields contain the OLE object pointer and the object's storage, respectively. CONTAIN has to fill in the ole_sto field, but the OLE libraries provide the pointer to the OLE object.

The flags field can store information about the object. In CONTAIN2, the only valid bit is bit 0. If bit 0 is set, the object is open in a server's window.

The next two fields are the public parts of CONTAIN's two interfaces. When you pass an interface to OLE, it expects a pointer to a pointer to the VTBL (this mimics how C++ compilers build VTBLs). Therefore, when CONTAIN wants to refer to its IClientSite interface, it can use &obj->cs_interface.

Recall from Chapter 6 that all interface functions receive the interface pointer as their first argument (the hidden this argument in C++). CONTAIN can cast the interface pointer into an _cs_interface or _as_interface pointer and then read the address of its private data structure from the object field.

The last field in the DOCOBJECT structure is the dtype variable. The dtype field stores the object's **aspect**—that is, how OLE renders the object. OLE allows you to request different aspects when you draw an object. For example, DVASPECT_CONTENT draws the contents of an object, and DVASPECT_ICON shows its icon. There are other aspects that some objects may support, but CONTAIN uses only these two.

The doc_info structure also grows with CONTAIN2. Since each object needs a unique name, doc_info contains a 32-bit unsigned integer that it uses to form object names. Of course, if you create more than four billion objects in one document, this won't work; it should be adequate for CONTAIN.

Providing an Interface

Writing an interface is not difficult. First, you refer to the OLE documentation to find out what functions the interface requires. Armed with that list, you write functions that do the required work. Next, you set the VTBL to point to the functions in the correct order.

Luckily, many OLE interface functions have trivial implementations. CONTAIN2 implements seventeen interface functions for two interfaces. Since both interfaces support IUnknown, three of these functions are the same for both interfaces and eight functions are just stubs. In addition, four of the functions are extremely simple to write. Thus, there are only a few functions of substance to write, and even they are not very difficult.

Writing Interface Functions

OLE2.H provides two macros for declaring OLE interface functions. STDMEHODIMP is for ordinary functions that return an HRESULT. For example:

```
STDMETHODIMP ClientSite_RequestNewObjectLayout(
    LPOLECLIENTSITE this)
```

```
{
return NOERROR;
}
```

Some functions don't return an HRESULT, so you also need the STDMETHODIMP_() macro. For example, to declare a void interface function, use the following:

```
STDMETHODIMP_(void) AdviseSink_OnClose(
   LPADVISESINK this)
   {
   }
```

Here is a typical function to implement the AddRef() function for the IUnknown interface:

```
#define GETOBJPTR(this) \
  (((struct _cs_interface FAR *)this)->object)


STDMETHODIMP_(ULONG) ConAddRef(LPVOID this)
  {
  DOCOBJECT *obj=GETOBJPTR(this);
  return ++(obj->refct);
  }
```

The GETOBJPTR macro converts the generic this pointer into a CONTAIN DOCOBJECT pointer. Most interface functions use this macro to obtain a pointer to CONTAIN's private data. Of course, you could compute a pointer to the data with address arithmetic, but this method is more direct and convenient. Listing 7-1 shows the CON_IF.C file, which defines CONTAIN's interface functions.

Listing 7-1. CON_IF.C

```c
/* CONTAIN Interface functions */
#include <windows.h>
#include "contain.h"
#include "c_ole.h"
#include <stdlib.h>


/* Convert THIS pointer to DOCOBJECT pointer */
#define GETOBJPTR(this) (((struct _cs_interface FAR *)\
                          this)->object)



/* **** IUnknown interface elements */

STDMETHODIMP ConQueryInterface(LPVOID this,REFIID iid,
             LPVOID FAR* new)
    {
    DOCOBJECT *obj=GETOBJPTR(this);
/* IClientSite? */
    if (IsEqualIID(iid, &IID_IOleClientSite))
      *new = &obj->cs_interface;
/* IAdviseSink? */
    else if (IsEqualIID(iid, &IID_IAdviseSink))
      *new = &obj->as_interface;
/* Huh? */
    else
      return ResultFromScode(E_NOINTERFACE);
/* Add ref it */
    AddRef((LPUNKNOWN)*new);
    return NOERROR;
    }
```

```
/* Generic AddRef */
STDMETHODIMP_(ULONG) ConAddRef(LPVOID this)
  {
  DOCOBJECT *obj=GETOBJPTR(this);
  return ++(obj->refct);
  }


/* Generic Release */
STDMETHODIMP_(ULONG) ConRelease(LPVOID this)
  {
  ULONG ret;
  DOCOBJECT *obj=GETOBJPTR(this);
  ret=--(obj->refct);
/* If no references, free object */
  if (!ret)
    {
    Release(obj->ole_obj);
    Release(obj->obj_sto);
    free(obj);
    }
  return ret;
  }


/* **** IClientSite Functions */

/* IClientSite::SaveObject() */
STDMETHODIMP ClientSite_SaveObject(LPOLECLIENTSITE this)
  {
  DOCOBJECT *obj=GETOBJPTR(this);
  LPPERSISTSTORAGE persistant;
  HRESULT rv;
  persistant=(LPPERSISTSTORAGE)OleStdQueryInterface(
```

```
                (LPUNKNOWN)obj->ole_obj,
                &IID_IPersistStorage);
  if (!persistant)
    return ResultFromScode(E_FAIL);
/* Make OLE save object */
  rv=OleSave(persistant,obj->obj_sto,TRUE);
  return rv!=S_OK?ResultFromScode(E_FAIL):NOERROR;
  }


/* IClientSite_GetMoniker() -- ignore for now */
STDMETHODIMP ClientSite_GetMoniker(LPOLECLIENTSITE this,
                                   DWORD assign,
                                   DWORD which,
                                   LPMONIKER FAR *ppmk)

  {
  *ppmk=NULL;
  return ResultFromScode(E_FAIL);
  }


/* IClientSite_GetContainer() -- don't need to respond
   to this */
STDMETHODIMP ClientSite_GetContainer(LPOLECLIENTSITE this,
                        LPOLECONTAINER FAR *contain)
   {
/* Don't know... */
   *contain=NULL;
   return ResultFromScode(E_FAIL);
   }


/* IClientSite::ShowObject() -- ignore */
STDMETHODIMP ClientSite_ShowObject(LPOLECLIENTSITE this)
  {
```

```
  return NOERROR;
  }


/* IClientSite::OnShowWindow()
   Notification from server */
STDMETHODIMP ClientSite_OnShowWindow(LPOLECLIENTSITE this,
                                      BOOL show)
  {
  DOCOBJECT *obj=GETOBJPTR(this);
  if (show)
    obj->flags|=OBJ_WINOPEN;
  else
    obj->flags&=~OBJ_WINOPEN;
  InvalidateRect(topwindow,&obj->bound,TRUE);
  return NOERROR;
  }


/* IClientSite::RequestNewObjectLayout() -- ignore */
STDMETHODIMP ClientSite_RequestNewObjectLayout(
                         LPOLECLIENTSITE this)
  {
  return NOERROR;
  }



/* ****Advise Sink functions */

/* IAdviseSink::OnDataChange() -- ignore */
STDMETHODIMP_(void) AdviseSink_OnDataChange(
                          LPADVISESINK this,
                          FORMATETC FAR *format_etc,
                          STGMEDIUM FAR *stg_med)
```

```
    {
    }


/* IAdviseSink::OnViewChange() -- redisplay view */
STDMETHODIMP_(void) AdviseSink_OnViewChange(
                                LPADVISESINK this,
                                DWORD dwAspect,
                                LONG lIndex)
    {
    DOCOBJECT *obj=GETOBJPTR(this);
    SIZEL p,m;
    HDC dc=GetDC(topwindow);
    RECT old;
    dirty=1;
/* Get new object size */
    GetExtent(obj->ole_obj,obj->dtype,&m);
    XformSizeInHimetricToPixels(dc,&m,&p);
    ReleaseDC(topwindow,dc);
    old=obj->bound;
    obj->bound.right=obj->bound.left+p.cx;
    obj->bound.bottom=obj->bound.top+p.cy;
/* We need to invalidate both the old and new bounds.
   The old bound needs erasing or needs to redraw
   what was under the object. */
/* redraw old bounding rectangle */
    InvalidateRect(topwindow,&old,TRUE);
/* Invalidate new bounding rectangle */
    InvalidateRect(topwindow,&obj->bound,TRUE);
    }


/* IAdviseSink::OnRename() -- ignore */
STDMETHODIMP_(void) AdviseSink_OnRename(LPADVISESINK this,
```

```
                                       LPMONIKER monik)
  {
  }


/* IAdviseSink::OnSave() -- ignore */
STDMETHODIMP_(void) AdviseSink_OnSave(LPADVISESINK this)
  {
  }


/* IAdviseSink::OnClose() -- see note below */
STDMETHODIMP_(void) AdviseSink_OnClose(LPADVISESINK this)
  {
/* Make sure flag gets cleared -- this is usually done in
   OnShowWindow(FALSE), but apparently some OLE 1.0
   objects have trouble here --  this makes sure. */
  DOCOBJECT *obj=GETOBJPTR(this);
  obj->flags&=~OBJ_WINOPEN;
  }



/* Vtables */
/* You can expect to get compiler warnings for the
   IUnknown functions -- don't worry about them */
IOleClientSiteVtbl contain_cs=
  {
  ConQueryInterface,
  ConAddRef,
  ConRelease,
  ClientSite_SaveObject,
  ClientSite_GetMoniker,
  ClientSite_GetContainer,
```

```
ClientSite_ShowObject,
ClientSite_OnShowWindow,
ClientSite_RequestNewObjectLayout
};


IAdviseSinkVtbl contain_as=
  {
  ConQueryInterface,
  ConAddRef,
  ConRelease,
  AdviseSink_OnDataChange,
  AdviseSink_OnViewChange,
  AdviseSink_OnRename,
  AdviseSink_OnSave,
  AdviseSink_OnClose
  };
```

CONTAIN must supply two interfaces: IClientSite and
IAdviseSink. Tables 7-1 and 7-2 show the functions these
interfaces require. Notice that many of these functions are
simple stubs.

Table 7-1. IClientSite Interface

Function	Implement	Description
SaveObject	Yes	Saves object to storage
GetMoniker	No[*]	Gets file moniker (for linking)
GetContainer	Stub	Gets container pointer
ShowObject	Stub	Shows object
OnShowWindow	Yes	Called on server open/close
RequestNewObjectLayout	Stub	Requests new layout

[*]Implemented later when CONTAIN does linking

Table 7-2. IAdviseSink Interface

Function	Implement	Description
OnDataChange	Stub	Data changed notification
OnViewChange	Yes	View changed notification
OnRename	Stub	Object renamed notification
OnSave	Stub	Object saved notification
OnClose	Yes	Object closing notification

The AddRef(), Release(), and QueryInterface() functions are the same for each interface. Also, many member functions are not necessary for CONTAIN (or most other container applications). You still have to supply these functions, but they don't do anything important.

The first routine that has any substance to it is the QueryInterface() function. This function simply compares the interface ID to the interfaces that CONTAIN supports (IID_IOleClientSite and IID_IAdviseSink). When it finds a match (by using the IsEqualIID() function), it returns a pointer to the interface.

OLE calls the IClientSite::SaveObject() function when it wants you to save the object to its storage. CONTAIN uses an OLE2UI function, OleStdQueryInterface(), to learn the OLE object's IPersistStorage interface. This function is simply a wrapper around the IUnknown::QueryInterface() call; you could just as well use the QueryInterface() macro from C_OLE.H.

Armed with the IPersistStorage interface, CONTAIN can use the OleSave() function to write the object to the storage. Again, CONTAIN lets OLE do most of the work.

The IClientSite::OnShowWindow() function informs CONTAIN when the object is opened in a server window or when the server window closes. CONTAIN updates its internal flag and marks the screen for redrawing, using InvalidateRect(). This allows CONTAIN to draw a shaded rectangle around the object when it is open.

The IAdviseSink::OnViewChange() function notifies CONTAIN that an object's appearance is now different. CONTAIN marks the file as dirty and invalidates the object to force a WM_PAINT message to occur.

Interface Initialization

When you construct an interface in C++, you don't need to initialize your interfaces—the C++ compiler does it for you. In C, you have to put the interface address functions in the VTBL. CONTAIN statically initializes the contain_cs and contain_as structures to point to the interface functions.

It's easier to initialize the table if you use some common-sense naming conventions. For example, CONTAIN uses ClientSite_SaveObject() for its IClientSite::SaveObject() function. Initializing the interface with this function is simple. Here is the interface declarations for CONTAIN:

```
IOleClientSiteVtbl contain_cs=
  {
  ConQueryInterface,
  ConAddRef,
  ConRelease,
  ClientSite_SaveObject,
  ClientSite_GetMoniker,
  ClientSite_GetContainer,
  ClientSite_ShowObject,
  ClientSite_OnShowWindow,
```

```
ClientSite_RequestNewObjectLayout
};

IAdviseSinkVtbl      contain_as=
  {
  ConQueryInterface,
  ConAddRef,
  ConRelease,
  AdviseSink_OnDataChange,
  AdviseSink_OnViewChange,
  AdviseSink_OnRename,
  AdviseSink_OnSave,
  AdviseSink_OnClose
};
```

Managing Objects

CONTAIN uses some simple functions (see Listing 7-2) to manage its linked list of objects. The make_object() function creates an uninitialized object. You can use add_obj() and del_obj() to add the object to the list or delete it.

Listing 7-2. CON_OBJ.C

```
/* Ole related functions for CONTAIN */
#include <windows.h>
#include "contain.h"
#include "c_ole.h"
#include <stdio.h>   /* for sprintf() */
#include <stdlib.h>


/* Insert object using OLE2UI dialog */
DOCOBJECT *ins_object(RECT *r)
  {
```

```
  OLEUIINSERTOBJECT oleins;
  DOCOBJECT *obj;
  char file[66];
  UINT rv;
/* Set up OLEUIINSERTOBJECT structure */
  memset(&oleins,0,sizeof(oleins));
  oleins.cbStruct=sizeof(oleins);
  oleins.hWndOwner=topwindow;
  *file='\0';
  oleins.lpszFile=file;
  oleins.cchFile=sizeof(file);
/* make "blank" object */
  obj=make_object(r,doc_info.objnr++);
/* Make storage */
  hresult=CreateStorage(main_sto,obj->objname,
              STD_ACCESS|STGM_CREATE,NULL,NULL,
              &obj->obj_sto);
  errck(7,0);
  onerr({ free(obj); doc_info.objnr--; return NULL; });
/* Set flags so OLE2UI will create object for us */
  oleins.dwFlags=IOF_DISABLELINK|IOF_SELECTCREATENEW
                |IOF_CREATENEWOBJECT|IOF_CREATEFILEOBJECT;
/* Ask for OLEOBJECT interface */
  oleins.iid=IID_IOleObject;
  oleins.oleRender=OLERENDER_DRAW;
  oleins.lpIOleClientSite=
     (LPOLECLIENTSITE)&obj->cs_interface;
  oleins.lpIStorage=obj->obj_sto;
  oleins.ppvObj=(LPVOID FAR *)&obj->ole_obj;
  rv=OleUIInsertObject(&oleins);
/* If call failed or was canceled, return */
  if (rv!=OLEUI_OK||oleins.sc!=S_OK)
    {
```

```
      free(obj);
      doc_info.objnr--;
      return NULL;
      }
/* hook new object into DOCOBJECT chain */
   add_obj(obj);
/* If iconic, switch aspect */
   if (oleins.dwFlags&IOF_CHECKDISPLAYASICON)
      {
      BOOL update;
      OleStdSwitchDisplayAspect(obj->ole_obj,
                  &obj->dtype,DVASPECT_ICON,
                  oleins.hMetaPict,FALSE,FALSE,
                  NULL,&update);
      if (oleins.hMetaPict)
        {
        OleStdSetIconInCache(obj->ole_obj,
                            oleins.hMetaPict);
        OleUIMetafilePictIconFree(oleins.hMetaPict);
        }
      }
/* Setup object advises */
   OleStdSetupAdvises(obj->ole_obj,obj->dtype,"CONTAIN",
     *filename?filename:"Untitled",
     (LPADVISESINK)&obj->as_interface,TRUE);
/* Activate new objects only */
   if (oleins.dwFlags&IOF_SELECTCREATENEW)
      obj_verb(obj,OLEIVERB_OPEN);
/* mark for redraw */
   invalid_obj(obj);
   return obj;
   }
```

```
/* Create unlinked object w/o storage or ole id */
DOCOBJECT *make_object(RECT *r,DWORD nr)
   {
   DOCOBJECT *rv;
   rv=malloc(sizeof(DOCOBJECT));
   if (!rv) return NULL;
/* Don't use wsprintf here --
   it doesn't handle the 08lx flag */
   sprintf(rv->objname,"OBJ%08lx",nr);
   rv->refct=1;
   rv->flags=0;
   rv->bound=*r;
   rv->ole_obj=NULL;
   rv->obj_sto=NULL;
   rv->next=rv->prev=NULL;
   rv->cs_interface.lpVtbl=&contain_cs;
   rv->cs_interface.object=rv->as_interface.object=rv;
   rv->as_interface.lpVtbl=&contain_as;
   rv->dtype=DVASPECT_CONTENT;
   return rv;
   }


/* Add object to linked list */
void add_obj(DOCOBJECT *obj)
   {
   DOCOBJECT *p=dochead;
   if (!p)
     {
/* First entry */
     dochead=obj;
     obj->next=obj->prev=NULL;
     }
   else
```

```
    {
/* find end of list */
    while (p->next) p=p->next;
/* append */
    p->next=obj;
    obj->next=NULL;
    obj->prev=p;
    }
  }


/* Remove object from list but don't destroy it */
void remove_obj(DOCOBJECT *obj)
  {
  if (obj==dochead)
    {
    dochead=obj->next;
    dochead->prev=NULL;
    }
  else
    {
    if (obj->prev) obj->prev->next=obj->next;
    if (obj->next) obj->next->prev=obj->prev;
    }
  }
/* Destroy object, removing from list if req'd */
void del_obj(DOCOBJECT *obj)
  {
  remove_obj(obj);
  if (obj->obj_sto) Release(obj->obj_sto);
  if (obj->ole_obj) Release(obj->ole_obj);
  free(obj);
  }
```

```
/* Perform verb on object */
obj_verb(DOCOBJECT *obj,int verb)
  {
  hresult=DoVerb(obj->ole_obj,verb,
         NULL,(LPOLECLIENTSITE)&(obj->cs_interface),
         0,topwindow,&obj->bound);
  errck(8,0);
  invalid_obj(obj);
  return 1;
  }


/* Invalidate object (including select box) */
void invalid_obj(DOCOBJECT *obj)
  {
  RECT invalid;
  invalid=obj->bound;
  if (obj==select)
    InflateRect(&invalid,BORDER,BORDER);
  InvalidateRect(topwindow,&invalid,TRUE);
  }
```

In response to the Insert Object command, CONTAIN calls the OLE2UI library from its ins_object() function. OLE2UI provides a standard dialog (see Figure 7-1) and can optionally create the object. Table 7-3 shows the parameters passed to OLE2UI (via the OLEUIINSERTOBJECT structure).

Note that the flag field in OLEUIINSERTOBJECT allows you to control the dialog before the call and obtain information after it returns. For example, the IOF_SELECTCREATE-FROMFILE bit (see Table 7-4) sets the initial state of the dialog so that it will create an object from a file. However, when the dialog completes, this bit is set if the user wants to create an object from a file.

Figure 7-1. The Insert Object Dialog

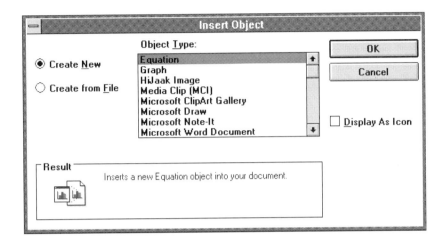

Table 7-3. OLEUIINSERTOBJECT Fields

Field	Type	Dir	Description
cbStruct	DWORD	In	Size of structure
dwFlags	DWORD	I/O	Flags (see Table 7-4)
hWndOwner	HWND	In	Owning window
lpszCaption	LPCSTR	In	Caption
lpfnHook	LPFNOLEUIHOOK	In	Hook callback
lCustData	LPARAM	In	Hook data
hInstance	HINSTANCE	In	Custom template instance
lpszTemplate	LPCSTR	In	Template name
hResource	HRSRC	In	Template handle
clsid	CLSID	I/O	Class ID
lpszFile	LPSTR	I/O	Filename for insert or link
cchFile	UINT	I/O	Size of lpszFile buffer
cClsidExclude	UINT	In	Number of CLSIDs to exclude

Table 7-3. OLEUIINSERTOBJECT Fields (continued)

Field	Type	Dir	Description
lpClsidExclude	LPCLSID	In	Array of excluded CLSIDs
iid	IID	In	Requested interface
oleRender	DWORD	In	Rendering option
lpFormatEtc	LPFORMATETC	In	Requested format
lpIOleClientSite	LPOLECLIENTSITE	In	Object's ClientSite
lpIStorage	PSTORAGE	In	Object's storage
ppvObj	LPVOID FAR *	I/O	Pointer to object's variable
sc	SCODE	Out	Result of create call
hMetaPict	HGLOBAL	Out	Icon (if necessary)

Table 7-4. OLEUIINSERTOBJECT Flags

Flag	Meaning
IOF_SHOWHELP	Shows help button
IOF_SELECTCREATENEW	Creates new selected
IOF_SELECTCREATEFROMFILE	Creates from file selected
IOF_CHECKLINK	Links check box checked
IOF_CHECKDISPLAYASICON	Icon check box checked
IOF_CREATENEWOBJECT	Allows new object creation
IOF_CREATEFILEOBJECT	Allows file insert creation
IOF_CREATELINKOBJECT	Allows link creation
IOF_DISABLELINK	Disables link option
IOF_VERIFYSERVERSEXIST	Verifies servers exists

CONTAIN sets the IOF_CREATENEWOBJECT flag, which allows the insert dialog code to go ahead and create the object for CONTAIN. If CONTAIN did not set the flag, it would be responsible for creating the new object based on the information OLE2UI returns in the structure and the OLEUIINSERTOBJECT fields from iid to hMetaPict would not be used. Usually, it is much easier to let OLE2UI do the work. The library call places the object in the variable you point to with the ppvObj field. The error code from the creation is in the sc field.

CONTAIN builds an uninitialized DOCOBJECT structure to hold the new OLE object. Once the OleUIInsertObject() function returns, CONTAIN takes the following steps:

- Call add_obj() to add the new DOCOBJECT to the linked list.

- Use the OLE2UI function OleStdSetupAdvises() to register CONTAIN's application and file names. Servers use this name in their menus and title bars. OleStdSetupAdvises() also registers CONTAIN's advise sink interface.

- Call obj_verb() to start the object's server (use the OLEIVERB_OPEN verb). This function uses the IOleObject::DoVerb() call.

- Use CONTAIN's invalid_obj() function to force the object to redraw. The only difference between invalid_obj() and InvalidateRect() is that invalid_obj() knows about the dashed box CONTAIN draws around the selected object. If you invalidate the selected object, invalid_obj() expands the rectangle to include the select box.

If OleUIInsertObject() returns with the IOF_CHECKDISPLAY-ASICON flag set, CONTAIN must do some additional work to cause OLE to display the icon instead of the object's contents. First, CONTAIN uses the OleStdSwitchDisplayAspect() function to switch the object's aspect to DVASPECT_ICON.

(Remember, the aspect determines how the object is displayed.) This call takes a pointer to the dtype field in DOCOBJECT. As part of its task, it places DVASPECT_ICON in this field. Later, when CONTAIN paints the object, it will use this field to request the iconic presentation.

When OleUIInsertObject() returns a non-null hMetaPict field, CONTAIN must set this metafile icon into the object's presentation cache. OLE maintains this cache to speed up object display. CONTAIN uses the OLE2UI function OleStdSetIconInCache() to insert the icon into the cache.

Drawing Objects

Now that CONTAIN has the OLE object in a DOCOBJECT structure, the WM_PAINT handler (update() in Listing 7-3) must draw it. All OLE objects support the IViewObject interface. You can use QueryInterface() or OleStdQuery-Interface() to find the IViewObject interface. Then, calling IViewObject::Draw() renders the object. The arguments to IViewObject::Draw() include the aspect (the dtype field in DOCOBJECT), the device context, and a RECTL rectangle. RECTL rectangles are similar to a RECT struct except that RECTLs use 32-bit values. The values in the RECTL argument use the MM_HIMETRIC mapping mode.

Since CONTAIN allows OLE to do most of the work, it uses the OleDraw() call to render objects. This is just a wrapper around the IViewObject::Draw() function. However, OleDraw() takes fewer arguments, and you can use any mapping mode you like (CONTAIN uses MM_TEXT). OleDraw() also takes a regular RECT structure as an argument instead of a RECTL.

When an object is open (the flags field in DOCOBJECT is set to OBJ_WINOPEN), CONTAIN must draw a shaded pattern over it. This signals the user that the object is open. The OLE2UI function OleUIDrawShading() will draw this shading. Unlike most OLE drawing functions, OleUIDrawShading() uses an ordinary RECT rectangle and allows you to use whatever mapping mode is current for the device context.

Listing 7-3. The update() Routine from CONTAIN.C

```
/* Update screen in response to WM_PAINT messages */
void update(HWND w)
  {
  HDC dc;
  PAINTSTRUCT paint;
  DOCOBJECT *i;
  LPVIEWOBJECT viewobj;
  dc=BeginPaint(w,&paint);
/* Paint objects backwards to preserve "front to back"
   order */
  for (i=dochead;i&&i->next;i=i->next);
/* Walk list backwards */
  for (;i;i=i->prev)
    {
/* Ask OLE to draw object */
    OleDraw((LPUNKNOWN)i->ole_obj,i->dtype,dc,&i->bound);
/* If object is open, ask OLE2UI to shade it */
    if (i->flags&OBJ_WINOPEN)
      OleUIDrawShading(&i->bound,dc,
          OLEUI_SHADE_FULLRECT,0);
/* If this is the selected object, draw a box around it */
    if (i==select)
      {
      HBRUSH br;
      HPEN pn,oldpen;
      br=SelectObject(dc,GetStockObject(HOLLOW_BRUSH));
```

```
    oldpen=SelectObject(dc,
      pn=CreatePen(PS_DASH,1,RGB(0,0,0)));
    Rectangle(dc,i->bound.left-BORDER,
      i->bound.top-BORDER,i->bound.right+BORDER,
      i->bound.bottom+BORDER);
/* Reset DC */
    SelectObject(dc,oldpen);
    SelectObject(dc,br);
    DeleteObject(pn);
    }
  }
  EndPaint(w,&paint);
  }
```

Loading and Saving Objects

CON_FILE.C (see Listing 7-4) provides functions to open and save files. Each file contains a stream named Contain and a substorage for each OLE object. The Contain stream holds the doc_info structure followed by each element of the DOCOBJECT list.

Listing 7-4. CON_FILE.C

```
/* File processing for CONTAIN */
#include <windows.h>
#include <string.h>
#include "contain.h"
#include "c_ole.h"
#include <commdlg.h>
#include <stdlib.h>


/* Close file */
int close_file()
```

```
  {
  DOCOBJECT *p,*nxt;
  if (main_sto)
    {
    /* prompt for save */
    if (dirty)
      {
      int n;
      n=MessageBox(topwindow,
                   "Save current document?","Confirm",
                   MB_YESNOCANCEL|MB_ICONQUESTION);
      if (n==IDCANCEL) return 0;
      if (n==IDYES) save_file(0);
      }
/* Walk document chain and free objects */
    for (p=dochead;p;p=nxt)
      {
      nxt=p->next;
      free(p);
      }
    dochead=NULL;
    dirty=0;
    *filename='\0';
    Release(main_sto);
    main_sto=NULL;
    }
  return 1;
  }

/* Create new file */
void new_file()
  {
  if (!close_file()) return;
```

```
/* Create temporary document file */
   hresult=StgCreateDocfile(NULL,
              STGM_CREATE|STD_ACCESS|
              STGM_DELETEONRELEASE,0,&main_sto);
   errck(1,0);
   onerr(return);
   dirty=dragging=currx=curry=0;
   select=NULL;
   set_title("Untitled");
   InvalidateRect(topwindow,NULL,TRUE);
   }

/* Open data file */
void open_file()
   {
   char title[66];
   struct _doc_info tmp;
   LPSTREAM str;
   DWORD cb;
   HRESULT rc;
   /* prompt for save or cancel */
   if (!close_file()) return;
   get_filename(title,sizeof(title),0);
   if (StgIsStorageFile(filename))
     {
     errck(3,0);   /* Error -- file is not structured */
     return;
     }
   hresult=StgOpenStorage(filename,NULL,STD_ACCESS,
                          NULL,0,&main_sto);
   errck(2,0);
   onerr(return);
```

```
/* Read doc_info & object list */

hresult=OpenStream(main_sto,"Contain",NULL,STD_ACCESS,0,&str);
   errck(3,0);
   onerr({ new_file(); return; });
   rc=Read(str,&tmp,sizeof(tmp),&cb);
   if (rc!=S_OK||cb!=sizeof(tmp)||tmp.magic!=0x8675309)
     {
     err(3,0);
     Release(str);
     new_file();
     return;
     }
   doc_info=tmp;
   ShowWindow(topwindow,SW_RESTORE);
/* Set window size as stored in file */
   SetWindowPos(topwindow,NULL,doc_info.r.left,
                doc_info.r.top,doc_info.r.right-
                doc_info.r.left,doc_info.r.bottom-
                doc_info.r.top,SWP_NOZORDER);
/* Read each object */
   do
     {
     DOCOBJECT dobj;
     rc=Read(str,&dobj,sizeof(DOCOBJECT),&cb);
     if (cb==sizeof(DOCOBJECT))
       {
       DOCOBJECT *el;
       DWORD nr;
       /* Find object # */
       nr=strtoul(dobj.objname+3,NULL,0x10);
       el=make_object(&dobj.bound,nr);
```

```
        if (!el) err(4,1);
        add_obj(el);
/* open storage */
        hresult=OpenStorage(main_sto,el->objname,
                    NULL,STD_ACCESS,NULL,NULL,
                    &el->obj_sto);
        errck(2,0);
//?      onerr();
/* make ole object from storage */
        hresult=OleLoad(el->obj_sto,&IID_IOleObject,
                    (LPOLECLIENTSITE)&el->cs_interface,
                    (LPVOID FAR *)&el->ole_obj);
        errck(2,0);
//        onerr();
/* Set up object info */
        OleStdSetupAdvises(el->ole_obj,DVASPECT_CONTENT,
            "CONTAIN",*filename?filename:"Untitled",
            (LPADVISESINK)&el->as_interface,TRUE);
        }
    } while (cb&&rc==S_OK);
  Release(str);
  dirty=dragging=currx=curry=0;
  select=NULL;
  InvalidateRect(topwindow,NULL,TRUE);
  set_title(title);
  }


/* Generic function to get a file name.
   Uses common dialogs. If how!=0 use Save,
   else use Open dialog */
get_filename(char *title,int len,int how)
  {
```

```
  OPENFILENAME fn;
  memset(&fn,0,sizeof(fn));
  fn.lStructSize=sizeof(fn);
  fn.hwndOwner=topwindow;
  fn.hInstance=hInst;
  fn.lpstrFilter="All Files\0*.*\0";
  fn.nFilterIndex=1;
  fn.lpstrFile=filename;
  fn.nMaxFile=sizeof(filename);
  fn.lpstrFileTitle=title;
  fn.nMaxFileTitle=len;
  fn.Flags=OFN_PATHMUSTEXIST;
  if (!how) fn.Flags|=OFN_FILEMUSTEXIST;
  return how?GetSaveFileName(&fn):GetOpenFileName(&fn);
  }


/* Save and save as */
void save_file(int flag)
  {
  LPSTREAM str;
  DOCOBJECT *list;
  if (flag||!*filename)  // save as
      {
/* On Save As, just make new storage and
   fall into ordinary save code */
      LPSTORAGE new;
      DOCOBJECT *p;
      char title[66];
      get_filename(title,sizeof(title),1);
      hresult=StgCreateDocfile(filename,STD_ACCESS,0,&new);
      errck(5,0);
      onerr(return);
```

```
/* Copy contents */
    hresult=CopyTo(main_sto,NULL,NULL,NULL,new);
    errck(6,0);
    onerr({ Release(new); return; });
/* Update DOCOBJECT list to reflect new
   storage */
    for (p=dochead;p;p=enum_docobject(p))
      {
      if (p->obj_sto) Release(p->obj_sto);
      hresult=OpenStorage(new,p->objname,NULL,
             STD_ACCESS,NULL,NULL,&p->obj_sto);
      errck(6,0);
      onerr({ Release(new); return; });
/* Set up object info */
      OleStdSetupAdvises(p->ole_obj,DVASPECT_CONTENT,
        "CONTAIN",*filename?filename:"Untitled",
        (LPADVISESINK)&p->as_interface,TRUE);
      }
    Release(main_sto);
    main_sto=new;
    set_title(title);
    }
/* main save code here */
  hresult=CreateStream(main_sto,"Contain",STD_ACCESS|
           STGM_CREATE,NULL,NULL,&str);
  errck(5,0);
  onerr(return);
  GetWindowRect(topwindow,&doc_info.r);
  hresult=Write(str,&doc_info,sizeof(doc_info),NULL);
  errck(6,0);
  onerr({ Release(str); return; });
  for (list=dochead;list;list=enum_docobject(list))
```

```
    {
    hresult=Write(str,list,sizeof(DOCOBJECT),NULL);
    errck(6,0);
    onerr({ Release(str); return; });
    }
  Release(str);
  dirty=0;
  }
```

File Operations Are Different with OLE

Most ordinary programs open a file, read it, and then close it. To save the file, these programs just write a new copy of it. OLE programs can't easily use this method of processing files.

Since each OLE object needs an open storage at all times, an OLE program must always have an open storage. Even a new document needs a storage. The new_file() function calls StgCreateDocfile() with a NULL file name. This creates a temporary storage that is suitable for a new document.

Although opening and saving a file is straightforward, saving a file to a new name is more difficult. CONTAIN uses StgCreateDocfile() to make a new file and uses the IPersistStorage::CopyTo() function to copy the current storage to the new one; all of the storages in the DOCOBJECT list now point to the old document. CONTAIN's save_file() function has to scan the list, calling Release() for each open storage and opening the new storage.

An Alternate Approach

OLE allows you to create storages from memory or even put them in custom storage items (like a database, for example). By using these non-file storages, you can incorporate OLE objects into your own data files.

For example, if you open a storage on a block of global memory, you can store it in your private file format by writing the global memory block. Still, unless you are particularly tied to a special file format, it makes more sense to use OLE's storage functions. You can elect to read ordinary files and OLE files, if you wish. The StgIsStorageFile() function can distinguish between an OLE file and other files. You can then read the file in whatever way is appropriate.

CONTAIN3—Running Verbs

CONTAIN2 performs the default verb when you double-click an object. Since many objects support only one verb anyway, this isn't much of a problem. However, if you are embedding sound, for example, you can play the sound but not edit it.

To access any verb, CONTAIN3 supports an Object menu. When you select an object, this menu contains verbs that apply to it. OLE provides an IEnumOLEVERB object that enumerates the verbs an object supports (see Chapter 6 for more about enumerators).

The enumerator returns an OLEVERB structure (see Table 7-5). Microsoft designed this structure with menus in mind, so you can use the fields directly in an AppendMenu() call. CONTAIN3 reserves menu IDs from IDM_OBJECT to IDM_OBJECT+99 (900-999) for the object menu. The object_-verbs() function (see Listing 7-5) adds IDM_OBJECT to each verb number and appends it to the Object menu. When the menu() function detects a verb menu selection, it simply subtracts IDM_OBJECT from the menu ID and passes the result to obj_verb().

Listing 7-5. The object_verbs() Function

```
/* Set up verb menu */
void object_verbs(DOCOBJECT *obj)
  {
  static int nrverbs=1;   /* 1 dummy item in menu */
  HMENU objmenu=GetSubMenu(GetMenu(topwindow),2);
  IEnumOLEVERB far *everb;
  OLEVERB verb;
/* Clear existing menu */
  while (nrverbs)
    DeleteMenu(objmenu,--nrverbs,MF_BYPOSITION);
/* If no selection or static, that's it */
  if (!obj) return;
/* Ask OLE for list of verbs */
  EnumVerbs(select->ole_obj,&everb);
  while (Next(everb,1,&verb,NULL)==S_OK)
    {
/* If verb belongs on menu... */
    if (verb.grfAttribs&2)
      {
      nrverbs++;
      AppendMenu(objmenu,verb.fuFlags,
          IDM_OBJECT+verb.lVerb,verb.lpszVerbName);
      }
    }
  Release(everb);
  }
```

Table 7-5. OLEVERB Structure

Field	Type	Description
lVerb	LONG	Verb number
lpszVerbName	LPSTR	Verb name
fuFlags	DWORD	AppendMenu() flags
grfAttribs	DWORD	Attributes
		1=verb never changes object
		2=verb should appear on menu

The menu_setup() function (in CONTAIN.C) calls object_verbs() while processing a WM_INITMENU message. This message occurs each time a menu is about to drop down. Later, menu_setup() will also enable and disable menu selections based on the state of the clipboard.

The first task object_verbs() does is to remove the previous object menu's entries. There is one dummy entry at start up (to satisfy the resource compiler), so object_verbs() initializes the nrverbs variable (a static integer) to one. This way, the first time the menu drops down, the dummy entry disappears. The function updates the nrverbs variable so that future calls to object_verbs() can remove the existing verb entries.

If you prefer a multilevel object menu (like the one found in Write, for example), you can use OleUIAddVerbMenu() from the OLE2UI library. This function takes an object, a menu, and a position in the menu. Figure 7-2 shows the OleUIAddVerbMenu() function and Figure 7-3 shows the type of menu it produces.

Figure 7-2. The OleUIAddVerbMenu() Function

```
BOOL OleUIAddVerbMenu(LPOLEOBJECT obj,LPSTR typ,
                  HMENU hmenu,UINT pos,
                  UINT min,BOOL cvtok,
                  UINT cvtid,HMENU FAR *cmenu);
```

where:

> obj - OLE object (NULL to disable verb menu).

> typ - Object's short type name. If NULL, OLE2UI will find the name.

> hmenu - Handle of menu to modify.

> pos - Position of verb menu item in hmenu.

> min - Menu ID of first verb. Subsequent verbs receive consecutive numbers.

> cvtok - TRUE to create a convert menu item.

> cvtid - If cvtok is TRUE, menu ID of convert item.

> cmenu - Pointer to handle of new menu.

Returns value:

Returns TRUE if menu created with one or more verbs; FALSE if call disabled menu.

Figure 7-3. Cascaded Verb Menu

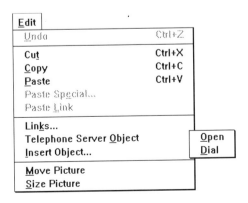

CONTAIN4—Using the Clipboard

OLE programs treat the clipboard differently than an ordinary application. As a result, to use the clipboard, CONTAIN must support a new interface, IDataObject. All OLE clipboard transactions are via data objects, which contain information about what data formats are available and how to get them. After you place the data object on the clipboard, other applications can retrieve this small object and then ask for the specific data they require.

You can also pass data by reference using data objects—that is, instead of transferring a copy of your data, you can tell the pasting application where the data resides (in a disk file, for instance).

Obviously, using a data object is more efficient than putting every possible format on the clipboard. You can think of data objects as an advanced form of delayed rendering (see Chapter 2).

Two data structures are central to the data object technique: FORMATETC and STGMEDIUM. The FORMATETC structure (see Table 7-6) is a generalization of a clipboard format. The STGMEDIUM (see Table 7-7) is what stands in for actual clipboard data. In other words, where you would ordinarily use a clipboard format (like CF_DIB), you now use a FORMATETC structure. When you receive data from a data object, you get a STGMEDIUM instead of a global handle.

Implementing a complete data object is quite complex. In theory, it should accept and render data in all formats. In practice, you only need to write a manageable subset of the data object. CONTAIN needs only a data object that supports data reads (IDataObject::GetData() and related functions). The IDataObject::SetData() function and all that support it are not necessary here.

Table 7-6. FORMATETC Fields

Field	Type	Description
cfFormat	CLIPFORMAT	Clipboard format
ptd	DVTARGETDEVICE FAR *	Target device
dwAspect	DWORD	Aspect (see Table 7-8)
lindex	LONG	Always -1 in OLE 2.0
tymed	DWORD	Media type (see Table 7-9)

Table 7-7. STGMEDIUM Fields

Field	Type	Description
tymed	DWORD	Media type (see Table 7-9)
u.hGlobal[*]	HANDLE	Generic Handle
u.lpszFileName[*]	LPSTR	File name
u.pstm[*]	IStream FAR *	Stream
u.pstg[*]	IStorage FAR *	Storage
pUnkForRelease	IUNKNOWN	Release interface for data

[*]If nameless unions are in use, omit u. (see text).

More About FORMATETC

The FORMATETC structure indicates a desired data format via its cfFormat field. This field contains an ordinary clipboard format identifier (like CF_TEXT) or the return value from a RegisterClipboardFormat() call.

The data request can also specify a device for rendering (the ptd field). This is usually NULL (indicating the screen device), although it may be a printer device if your program prints. The dwAspect and lindex fields specify the data's aspect. These are nearly always DVASPECT_CONTENT and -1, respectively. This format is the normal view of the data. Contrast this with the other aspects: DVASPECT_THUMBNAIL, DVASPECT_ICON, and DVASPECT_DOCPRINT. Of course, many data items support only DVASPECT_CONTENT, anyway.

Finally, the tymed field can contain multiple bit values for the type of return medium needed (see Table 7-8). If more than one media type is acceptable, the values are or'ed together. Again, some data object may elect only to render a format in certain media. These bits indicate which format the caller will accept. Your data object then looks at a FORMATETC structure and decides if it can process the request or not. If it can, it returns data in a STGMEDIUM structure.

The OLE headers provide two macros to simplify creating FORMATETC structures. The SETFORMATETC() macro allows you to set all the fields in a FORMATETC structure with one pseudo-function call. Another macro, SETDEFAULT-FORMATETC(), lets you set two fields: cfFormat and tymed. The remaining fields receive their most frequent values (dwAspect=DVASPECT_CONTENT, ptd=NULL, and lindex=-1).

Table 7-8. DVASPECT Values

Value	Description	lindex value
DVASPECT_CONTENT	Object contents	always -1
DVASPECT_THUMBNAIL	Reduced view	ignored
DVASPECT_ICON	Iconic view	ignored
DVASPECT_DOCPRINT	Printer view	-1 or page[*]

[*]Pages not currently supported by OLE 2.0.

More About STGMEDIUM

The STGMEDIUM structure contains a tymed field, a union, and a pointer to an IUnknown interface pointer. The tymed field has a single medium-type value that indicates how the data is available in the data union (see Table 7-9). By examining the tymed field, the caller can decide which union member to read.

Table 7-9. TYMED Values

Value	Description
TYMED_HGLOBAL	Global memory block
TYMED_FILE	File
TYMED_ISTREAM	OLE stream
TYMED_ISTORAGE	OLE storage
TYMED_GDI	GDI object (e.g., bitmap)
TYMED_MFPICT	Metafile Picture
TYMED_NULL	None

The union can contain a file name, a handle, or an IStorage or IStream. If your compiler supports nameless unions, the OLE libraries leave this union unnamed. This allows you to omit the union's tag when using one of its fields. For example:

```
STGMEDIUM s;
s.hGlobal=glob_hndl;
```

However, strict ANSI C doesn't allow nameless unions. If you define NONAMELESSUNION before compiling your program, OLE assigns the union a tag of u. You then write the above example like this:

```
STGMEDIUM s;
s.u.hGlobal=glob_hndl;
```

Since some compilers do not support nameless unions, all the code in this book uses NONAMELESSUNION. However, if you look at other OLE code, you may see the nameless union convention.

Usually, you want to pass a copy of your data in the STGMEDIUM that is strictly for the caller to use (just as you pass copies of data on the ordinary clipboard). You can then set the pUnkForRelease field to NULL. When pUnkForRelease is NULL, the caller knows it can release the object at will. If you want to share an object between yourself and others, you can set pUnkForRelease to an interface pointer. The caller then releases this interface pointer when it is done with the contents of the storage medium.

The IDataObject Interface

The DataObject interface contains nine functions (not including the usual three for IUnknown—see Table 7-10). In this case, five are just stubs and OLE2UI handles one for you. This leaves three functions to actually implement.

You can use an internal OLE2UI function to write the IDataObject::EnumFormatEtc() function (see DataObject_-EnumFormatEtc() in CON_IF.C). Users of your data object call this function to get an enumerator (see Chapter 5) that lists the data formats it might support. Just because the object returns a value via this enumeration doesn't mean it guarantees that it supports that format; however, it shouldn't support formats not on this list.

Table 7-10. The IDataObject Interface

Function	Implement	Description
GetData	Yes	Gets data in new medium
GetDataHere	Yes	Gets data in existing medium
QueryGetData	Yes	Sees if data available
GetCanonicalFormatEtc	Stub	Finds equivalent format
SetData	Stub	Sets data into object
EnumFormatEtc	OLE2UI	Enumerates formats
DAdvise	Stub	Sets up advise loop
DUnadvise	Stub	Stops advise loop
EnumDAdvise	Stub	Lists active advise loops

For CONTAIN's simple purposes, it can steal the enumerator object from OLE2UI. If the caller requests formats that it can set into the data object, CONTAIN returns E_FAIL. Otherwise, it calls OleStdEnumFmtEtc_Create(). This library call does all the work of defining and managing an enumeration class that contains the formats CONTAIN needs.

The first real function to implement is IDataObject::-QueryGetData(). This function examines a FORMATETC structure and returns NOERROR if the object can satisfy the request. Otherwise, it returns DATA_E_FORMATETC. Note that it doesn't return data—it just indicates if the request would succeed.

CONTAIN maintains a list of formats it supports (the get_fmts[] array). It compares the formats it supports with the prospective format. If there is a match, the QueryGetData() call succeeds. If not, CONTAIN calls QueryGetData() for the OLE object contained in the data object (if any). If the object can supply the data, the call succeeds. Otherwise, QueryGetData() fails for that FORMATETC.

The IDataObject::GetData() and IDataObject::GetDataHere() functions are very similar except that they return data to the caller. With GetData(), you are responsible for creating the STGMEDIUM that holds the data. With GetDataHere(), the caller supplies a STGMEDIUM.

In both cases, CONTAIN tries to pass the work off to the OLE object by calling its GetData() or GetDataHere() function. If that function fails, CONTAIN calls its obj_data() function to satisfy the request (see Listing 7-6).

Listing 7-6. The obj_data() Function

```
/* Try to get data for GetData and GetDataHere
   Returns 1 on success; 0 on failure */
static int obj_data(DOCOBJECT *obj,LPFORMATETC fmt,
                    LPSTGMEDIUM medium,int flag)
  {
  POINTL point;
  HGLOBAL glob;
  LPSTR data,rv;
  if (!flag)
    {
    medium->tymed=NULL;
    medium->u.hGlobal=NULL;
    medium->pUnkForRelease=NULL;
    }
/* We do text in HGLOBALs. The text is the
   user type (e.g., Microsoft Word Document) */
  if (fmt->cfFormat==CF_TEXT)
    {
    if (!(fmt->tymed&&TYMED_HGLOBAL))
```

```
        return 0;
    if (!flag)
      {
      glob=GlobalAlloc(GMEM_MOVEABLE|GMEM_ZEROINIT|
                       GMEM_SHARE,512);
      if (!glob)
        return 0;
      }
    else
      glob=medium->u.hGlobal;
    data=GlobalLock(glob);
    if (data)
      {
      hresult=GetUserType(obj->ole_obj,
             USERCLASSTYPE_FULL,&rv);
      if (hresult!=S_OK)
        lstrcpy(data,"Unknown OLE object");
      else
        lstrcpy(data,rv);
      GlobalUnlock(glob);
      }
    if (!flag)
      {
      medium->tymed=TYMED_HGLOBAL;
      medium->u.hGlobal=glob;
      }
    return 1;
    }
/* We do cf_object */
  else if (fmt->cfFormat==cf_object)
    {
    if (!(fmt->tymed&TYMED_HGLOBAL)) return 0;
    if (flag) return 0;
```

```
        point.x=point.y=0;
/* Long function to get object descriptor -- see
   text if you have problems compiling this */
      glob=OleStdGetObjectDescriptorDataFromOleObject(
              obj->ole_obj,NULL,
              obj->dtype,point,NULL);
      if (!glob) return 0;
      medium->tymed=TYMED_HGLOBAL;
      medium->u.hGlobal=glob;
      return 1;
      }
/* We do embedded objects */
  else if (fmt->cfFormat==cf_embedd)
    {
    if (!(fmt->tymed&TYMED_ISTORAGE)) return 0;
    if (!flag)
      StgCreateDocfile(NULL,
          STGM_CREATE|STD_ACCESS|STGM_DELETEONRELEASE,
          0,&medium->u.pstg);
    hresult=CopyTo(obj->obj_sto,NULL,NULL,NULL,
                   medium->u.pstg);
    return hresult==S_OK;
    }
/* We don't do anything else */
  return 0;
  }
```

The obj_data() function supports only certain combinations of formats and media; in practice, these are sufficient. The three formats it supports are CF_TEXT, object descriptors, and embedded objects. CONTAIN registers the last two formats (using RegisterClipboardFormat()) into the cf_object and cf_embedd variables.

For CF_TEXT, obj_data() calls GetUserType() to determine the object's type (for example, Microsoft Word Document). It places this text in the hGlobal field of the storage medium. If the call is GetData()—rather than GetDataHere()—obj_data() allocates the handle.

When the caller requests an object descriptor, CONTAIN passes off the dirty work to OLE2UI again. The OleStdGetObjectDescriptorDataFromOleObject() call is not only a mouthful, but it does the hard work required to get the object descriptor.

If you use a C compiler with limited name length, you may have trouble calling OleStdGetObjectDescriptorData-FromOleObject(). You have two options you can try: 1) Use an IMPORTS section in your module definition file to rename the long symbol or 2) Modify the source for OLE2UI to give this function a more reasonable name. For example, if you use Borland C++, CONTAIN.DEF should have these lines in it:

```
IMPORTS
    OLESTDGETOBJECTDESCRIPTORDATAFRO=
        OLEUI.OLESTDGETOBJECTDESCRIPTORDATAFROMOLEOBJECT
```

You'll find more information about this problem in the Appendix.

When the caller wants the embedded object format, CONTAIN copies the object's structured storage to a different IStorage. Again, if the call was GetData(), CONTAIN creates this storage. Otherwise, it uses the storage passed by the caller.

Putting It Together

Armed with a data object implementation, CONTAIN is ready to support cut, copy, and paste. These functions are in the obj_clip() function (see CON_OBJ.C and Listing 7-7). The cut command simply use OleSetClipboard() to put the object on the clipboard. It then removes the object from CONTAIN's list.

This method won't work for copying data. When you place an object on the clipboard, you expect it to be a snapshot of the object at that time. If you paste the actual object into another application, it reflects the object's state that the time of the paste operation—not the time of the copy. CONTAIN handles this by making an invisible copy of the object and cutting the copy.

Pasting is more complex. The paste code calls OleGetClipboard(). This function returns a data object that represents the contents of the clipboard. OleGetClipboard can return a data object even if the source of the data is not an OLE 2 application. The OLE libraries synthesize data objects for OLE 1 objects, bitmaps, and metafiles. CONTAIN doesn't care where the data originates.

Once CONTAIN has a data object, it creates an empty document object and a storage for the new item. It then uses the OleQueryCreateFromData() function to determine if the data object contains an OLE object. If there is no OLE object, CONTAIN calls OleCreateStaticFromData(). This creates a static object (that is, an ordinary bitmap or metafile). This is a handy way to get bitmaps and metafiles into a program since OLE handles all of the drawing issues.

If the data object contains a non-static OLE object, CONTAIN uses OleCreateFromData() to make the new object. This handles both OLE 1 and OLE 2 objects.

If CONTAIN had its own data formats, it would try to paste them first. If a private format was not available, then CONTAIN would try the OLE method. Of course, you could also extend CONTAIN's data object to support the private formats. You would then simply use QueryGetData() to determine if CONTAIN should use its own routines or one of the OleCreate functions.

Listing 7-7. The obj_clip() Function

```
/* Clipboard code. Handles:
   Cut, Copy, and Paste */
void obj_clip(int cmd)
  {
  LPDATAOBJECT data;
  DOCOBJECT *clip,*obj;
  switch (cmd)
    {
/* Cut is very simple, just move object to clipboard */
    case IDM_CUT:
      clip=select;
move2clip:
      data=NULL;
      OleSetClipboard((LPDATAOBJECT)&clip->do_interface);
      remove_obj(clip);
      break;


    case IDM_COPY:
/* make copy of object and jmp to move2clip */
      clip=make_object(&select->bound,
            strtoul(select->objname+3,NULL,0x10));
      StgCreateDocfile(NULL,
            STD_ACCESS|STGM_DELETEONRELEASE,0,
            &clip->obj_sto);
      CopyTo(select->obj_sto,NULL,NULL,
            NULL,clip->obj_sto);
      clip->ole_obj=select->ole_obj;
      AddRef(clip->ole_obj);
      goto move2clip;
/* Paste... */
    case IDM_PASTE:
```

```
      {
      RECT r;
      r.left=r.top=0;
      r.bottom=r.right=100;
      data=NULL;
      hresult=OleGetClipboard(&data);
      if (!SUCCEEDED(hresult)) return;
      obj=make_object(&r,doc_info.objnr++);
      hresult=CreateStorage(main_sto,obj->objname,
              STD_ACCESS|STGM_CREATE,NULL,NULL,
              &obj->obj_sto);
      errck(7,0);
/* Figure out which create to use */
      hresult=OleQueryCreateFromData(data);
      if (hresult==S_OK)
        hresult=OleCreateFromData(data,&IID_IOleObject,
                OLERENDER_DRAW,NULL,
                (LPOLECLIENTSITE)&obj->cs_interface,
                obj->obj_sto,
                (LPVOID FAR *)&obj->ole_obj);

      else if (hresult==(HRESULT)OLE_S_STATIC)
        {
        hresult=OleCreateStaticFromData(data,&IID_IOleObject,
                OLERENDER_DRAW,NULL,
                (LPOLECLIENTSITE)&obj->cs_interface,
                obj->obj_sto,(LPVOID FAR *)&
                obj->ole_obj);
        obj->flags|=OBJ_STATIC;
        }
      errck(7,0);
/* Set up object */
```

```
    OleStdSetupAdvises(obj->ole_obj,obj->dtype,"CONTAIN",
        *filename?filename:"Untitled",
        (LPADVISESINK)&obj->as_interface,TRUE);
    Release(data);
/* Add object to list */
    add_obj(obj);
/* Invalidate object */
    invalid_obj(obj);
    }
  }
 }
```

Managing Menus

CONTAIN should enable the Paste option in the Edit menu only when there is something on the clipboard. Similarly, the Cut and Copy commands are available only when there is some object selected. CONTAIN uses the menu_setup() function in CONTAIN.C to manage the menu. The WM_INITMENU message calls this function.

The Cut and Copy commands are active only when the select variable is not NULL. Several other menu selections work the same way. A simple call to EnableMenuItem() either enables or grays each item.

The Paste item is gray unless OleGetClipboard() returns a data item and OleQueryCreateFromData() succeeds. Note that CONTAIN uses the SUCCEEDED() macro to test the return from OleQueryCreateFromData(). If it simply tested for S_OK, it would fail to enable the Paste command when the clipboard contained a static object (OLE_S_STATIC).

Be sure to release the data pointer that OleGetClipboard() returns so that OLE knows to close the clipboard for you.

CONTAIN5—Linking

Since CONTAIN uses the OLE2UI functions to create new items, linking is quite simple. You need only one additional piece of data—a moniker—to allow CONTAIN to properly interact with a linking server.

Monikers

Linking has one problem not present in embedding: locating the source file. OLE stores a full path name to the linked file in a moniker. This **moniker** is a data structure that identifies a file location; it also contains information meaningful to the link source. For example, it might contain a file name for a spreadsheet and range of cells within the spreadsheet.

Suppose that a user creates a link to another document in the same directory, then moves both files to another directory on a laptop. Since the file path is no longer the same, OLE can't find the linked document.

To combat this problem, OLE also uses relative monikers, which contain the path required to change from the document's directory to the link source's directory. In the preceding example, the relative moniker would be . (plus any additional link-specific information). Absolute and the relative monikers give OLE a better chance of locating a link source when things are moved around.

Creating a Moniker for CONTAIN

Since the linking server must form a relative moniker, it needs a moniker that describes CONTAIN's document location. Since CONTAIN manages only a single document, it creates the moniker once when the file is first opened or saved. For a new file, CONTAIN calls the OLE2UI function, OleStdCreateTempFileMoniker(). If CONTAIN knows the file name, it uses CreateFileMoniker() instead. The IClientSite::GetMoniker() function must return the moniker

when it processes an OLEWHICHMK_CONTAINER request.
Listing 7-8 shows the important parts of this code.

Listing 7-8. IClientSite::GetMoniker() Function

```
/* IClientSite_GetMoniker()
   Retrieves document's moniker that linking
   servers need */
STDMETHODIMP ClientSite_GetMoniker(LPOLECLIENTSITE this,
                                   DWORD assign,
                                   DWORD which,
                                   LPMONIKER FAR *ppmk)
  {
  *ppmk=NULL;
/* Only need to handle OLEWHICHMK_CONTAINER */
  if (which==OLEWHICHMK_CONTAINER)
    *ppmk=monk;
  if (*ppmk)
    AddRef((*ppmk));
  return *ppmk?NOERROR:ResultFromScode(E_FAIL);
  }
```

CONTAIN6—Adding Paste Special

The Paste command tries to insert data in the most descriptive
format available. Many applications also provide a Paste
Special command. This command allows the user to view the
formats on the clipboard and select one for insertion. You can
also link to data using this command.

The OLE2UI library supplies a call to do most of the required
work for Paste Special. CONTAIN6 modifies the obj_clip()
command to call this function (OleUIPasteSpecial()). When
the function returns, obj_clip() sets a FORMATETC structure
based on the result of the call. It then jumps to the ordinary

paste code to do the actual insertion. When the ordinary Paste command executes, it sets the FORMATETC structure to NULL to fetch the default data type.

The paste logic in obj_clip() now needs to handle links and icons since these may result from the Paste Special command. Still, these changes are minimal—obj_clip() simply uses OleCreateLinkFromData() for links and modifies the aspect for iconic display (see the preceding description of ins_obj() for more details). Listing 7-9 shows the modified obj_clip() function.

Listing 7-9. Paste Special obj_clip() Function

```
/* Clipboard code.  Handles:
   Cut, Copy, Paste, and Paste Special */
void obj_clip(int cmd)
  {
  LPDATAOBJECT data;
  DOCOBJECT *clip,*obj;
  LPFORMATETC fmt=NULL;
  RECT r;
  int spcl_static=0;
  int icon=0;
  int link=0;
  switch (cmd)
    {
/* Cut is very simple, just move object to clipboard */
    case IDM_CUT:
      clip=select;
move2clip:
      data=NULL;
      OleSetClipboard((LPDATAOBJECT)&clip->do_interface);
      remove_obj(clip);
      break;
```

```
    case IDM_COPY:
/* make copy of object and jmp to move2clip */
      clip=make_object(&select->bound,
            strtoul(select->objname+3,NULL,0x10));
      StgCreateDocfile(NULL,
            STD_ACCESS|STGM_DELETEONRELEASE,0,
            &clip->obj_sto);
      CopyTo(select->obj_sto,NULL,NULL,
            NULL,clip->obj_sto);
      clip->ole_obj=select->ole_obj;
      AddRef(clip->ole_obj);
      goto move2clip;


/* Use OLE2UI for Paste Special */
    case IDM_PASTESPCL:
      {
      int i;
      OLEUIPASTESPECIAL olepaste;
      static int first=1;
      hresult=OleGetClipboard(&data);
      if (!SUCCEEDED(hresult)) return;
      if (first)
        {
/* One time set up */
        first=0;
        linkty[0]=cf_embedd;
        linkty[1]=cf_object;
        pasters[0].fmtetc=get_fmts[1];
        pasters[1].fmtetc.cfFormat=CF_METAFILEPICT;
        pasters[2].fmtetc.cfFormat=CF_DIB;
        pasters[3].fmtetc.cfFormat=CF_BITMAP;
        pasters[1].fmtetc.tymed=TYMED_MFPICT;
        pasters[3].fmtetc.tymed=
```

```
            pasters[2].fmtetc.tymed=TYMED_HGLOBAL;
        }
/* Set up common dialog structure */
    memset(&olepaste,0,sizeof(olepaste));
    olepaste.cbStruct=sizeof(olepaste);
    olepaste.hWndOwner=topwindow;
    olepaste.lpSrcDataObj=data;
    olepaste.arrPasteEntries=pasters;
    olepaste.cPasteEntries=PASTEENTRYS;
    olepaste.cLinkTypes=sizeof(linkty)/sizeof(UINT);
    olepaste.arrLinkTypes=linkty;
/* Call OLE2UI dialog */
    if (OleUIPasteSpecial(&olepaste)!=OLEUI_OK)
      return;
    if (olepaste.nSelectedIndex!=0)
      {
      spcl_static=1;
      fmt=&pasters[olepaste.nSelectedIndex].fmtetc;
      }
    else
      {
      spcl_static=-1;
/* get metafile for object formats */
      fmt=&pasters[1].fmtetc;
      }
    if (olepaste.dwFlags&PSF_CHECKDISPLAYASICON)
      icon=1;
    if (olepaste.dwFlags&PSF_SELECTPASTELINK)
      link=1;
/* Let ordinary paste code handle everything from here */
    goto pasteit;
    }
```

```
/* Paste... */
    case IDM_PASTE:
      {
      data=NULL;
      hresult=OleGetClipboard(&data);
      if (!SUCCEEDED(hresult)) return;
/* Entry point for PasteSpecial */
pasteit:
        r.left=r.top=0;
        r.bottom=r.right=100;
/* This code is very similar to ins_object() */
/* make blank object */
        obj=make_object(&r,doc_info.objnr++);
        hresult=CreateStorage(main_sto,obj->objname,
                  STD_ACCESS|STGM_CREATE,NULL,NULL,
                  &obj->obj_sto);
        errck(7,0);


/* Figure out which create to use */
        if (spcl_static==0)
          hresult=OleQueryCreateFromData(data);
        else if (spcl_static==-1)
          hresult=S_OK;
        else
          hresult=(HRESULT)OLE_S_STATIC;


        if (hresult==S_OK)
          if (link)
            hresult=OleCreateLinkFromData(data,&IID_IOleObject,
              fmt?OLERENDER_FORMAT:OLERENDER_DRAW,fmt,
              (LPOLECLIENTSITE)&obj->cs_interface, obj->obj_sto,
              (LPVOID FAR *)&obj->ole_obj);
          else
```

```
              hresult=OleCreateFromData(data,&IID_IOleObject,
                       fmt?OLERENDER_FORMAT:OLERENDER_DRAW,fmt,
                       (LPOLECLIENTSITE)&obj->cs_interface,
                       obj->obj_sto,
                       (LPVOID FAR *)&obj->ole_obj);

        else if (hresult==(HRESULT)OLE_S_STATIC)
          {
          hresult=OleCreateStaticFromData(data,&IID_IOleObject,
                       fmt?OLERENDER_FORMAT:OLERENDER_DRAW,
                       fmt,(LPOLECLIENTSITE)&obj->cs_interface,
                       obj->obj_sto,(LPVOID FAR *)&
                       obj->ole_obj);
          obj->flags|=OBJ_STATIC;
          }
        errck(7,0);
        if (hresult==S_OK)
          {
/* Switch display if iconic */
          if (icon)
            {
            BOOL update;
            OleStdSwitchDisplayAspect(obj->ole_obj,
                  &obj->dtype,DVASPECT_ICON,
                  NULL,FALSE,FALSE,NULL,
                  &update);
            }
/* Set up object */
          prep_obj(obj);
/* Add object to list */
          add_obj(obj);
/* Invalidate object */
```

```
        invalid_obj(obj);
        }
    else   // error!
        del_obj(obj);
    Release(data);
    }
  }
}
```

CONTAIN7—Adding Drag-and-Drop Support

One new OLE 2.0 feature is drag-and-drop. This provides a protocol for applications to transfer data objects without using the clipboard. From the user's point of view, here is what happens:

1. The user clicks on an object in a document and holds the mouse button down.

2. Windows changes the mouse cursor to an arrow with a small box attached (see Figure 7-4a) to indicate that the object will move if the user releases the mouse (that is, drops the object).

3. As the user drags the mouse, the cursor may change shape. A circle with a slash means the object cannot drop at the current location (Figure 7-4b). An arrow, box, and plus sign (Figure 7-4c) means that you may drop a copy of the object at the current location.

4. Releasing the mouse button causes the action to occur. If the cursor is a circle and slash, no operation takes place.

The user can usually hold down the shift key to force a move or the control key to force a copy operation.

Figure 7-4. Drag-and-Drop Cursors

(a) Move   (b) No Action   (c) Copy

You can use drag-and-drop to move and copy objects within your own application and to exchange objects with other participating applications. The protocol is very simple; as long as you can create and accept data objects, drag-and-drop is easy to implement.

Planning for Drag-and-Drop

Before implementing drag-and-drop, you need to decide how to handle internal dragging. From a code standpoint, it is simpler to let the OLE drag-and-drop code handle any movement of objects internal to your application. However, drag-and-drop is probably slower than your existing techniques. Also, you must take special pains to prevent OLE from dropping objects in the same place as they started. If you don't prevent this, an object will move every time the user clicks on it to select it.

Of course, using your own move code has problems, too. If you choose to use private code for internal moves, you must pass control to OLE when the cursor leaves your window. However, if the cursor moves back into the window, OLE will not return control to your code. This could be confusing to users and programmers alike.

CONTAIN7 uses OLE for all dragging. This allows you to compare it with the internal dragging from CONTAIN6 to get an idea of the performance penalties. Of course, the existing dragging code has to be removed before the new code can work.

The Drag-and-Drop Interfaces

Drag-and-drop requires two small interfaces: IDropSource and IDropTarget (see Tables 7-11 and 7-12). The IDropSource interface is for applications that want to provide objects and the IDropTarget interface is for programs that accept data. Usually, you implement both. These interfaces don't need to exist at the object level; you can implement one copy of each for your entire document.

Table 7-11. The IDropSource Interface

Function	Implement	Description
QueryContinueDrag	Yes	Stops drag or drop
GiveFeedback	Stub	Modifies drag cursor

Table 7-12. The IDropTarget Interface

Function	Implement	Description
DragEnter	Yes	Object entering window
DragOver	Yes[*]	Object moving in window
DragLeave	Stub	Object leaving window
Drop	Yes	Object dropped in window

[*] Same implementation as DragEnter().

For simplicity, CONTAIN7 adds the IDropSource interface to the existing document object (although the interface could be global and work with the select variable). However, IDropTarget must be independent. If it were not, you could not drop objects into an empty document.

Besides the two interfaces, there are three drag-and-drop APIs:

- RegisterDragDrop()—This function notifies OLE that a specific window will accept drops. You must pass the window handle and a pointer to the IDropTarget interface.

- RevokeDragDrop()—This call signals an end of a window's willingness to accept drops.

- DoDragDrop()—When a data source detects a drag operation beginning, it calls DoDragDrop(). OLE handles everything from that point. The arguments include pointers to the data object and the IDropSource interface. Another argument points to a DWORD where OLE places the results of the drag.

Drag-and-Drop Basics

OLE calls a drop target's DragEnter() function when the cursor first moves into its window. The target must respond with the action that would occur if the object dropped (usually DROPEFFECT_NONE, DROPEFFECT_MOVE, or DROPEFFECT_COPY). The DragOver() function is similar but occurs as the mouse moves over the window. Both calls receive the keyboard state and the mouse position as arguments. The DragEnter() function also gets a pointer to the data object. Some early OLE documentation states that the mouse position is in window coordinates. This is not correct; the mouse position is in screen coordinates.

When the cursor moves out of the window, OLE calls the target's DragLeave() function. This call usually does nothing, but you can use it if you have a complex setup in DragEnter().

The real action takes place in the Drop() function. At this point, the program must take the data object and insert it into the document at the mouse position. This is very similar to pasting from the clipboard, so you probably can reuse your clipboard code here.

From the drop source side, things are even simpler. The QueryContinueDrag() function can return one of three values:

- S_OK—Continue dragging
- DRAGDROP_S_CANCEL—Stop dragging
- DRAGDROP_S_DROP—Drop object at current position

QueryContinueDrag() determines what to return by examining the key state and the status of the escape key (both arguments sent by OLE). If the mouse button that initiated the drag is no longer pressed, the function should return DRAGDROP_S_DROP. If the escape key is down, it should return DRAGDROP_S_CANCEL. When none of these conditions apply, simply return S_OK.

The GiveFeedback() function is responsible for modifying the cursor based on the current drop effect. This seems like a lot of work, but luckily you can simply return DRAGDROP_S_-USEDEFAULTCURSORS, and OLE will do the dirty work for you.

Much of the work in drag-and-drop involves examining the current key state. Therefore, many drag-and-drop interface functions receive the keyboard state as an argument. You can test this value against the constants in Table 7-13.

Table 7-13. Drag-and-Drop Keystate Values

Value	Description
MK_LBUTTON	Left mouse button
MK_RBUTTON	Right mouse button
MK_MBUTTON	Middle mouse button
MK_ALT	Alt key
MK_CONTROL	Control key
MK_SHIFT	Shift key

Writing CONTAIN7

The implementation of drag-and-drop in CONTAIN is very simple. Of course, the RegisterDragDrop() and RevokeDragDrop() calls occur during startup and shutdown, respectively. Also, when a left mouse click occurs, CONTAIN calls DoDragDrop().

CONTAIN's drag-and-drop interface uses several global variables to retain state information:

- drop_data—Data object (destined for clipboard code)

- drop_rect—Where to place dropped object

- drop_local—Signal that object was dragged inside CONTAIN

- drop_start—Position drag began

- dragging—Signal that dragging began in CONTAIN

There are two special cases that CONTAIN must handle. First, if the mouse does not move during the drag operation,

CONTAIN should take no action. This prevents unnecessary movement when the user clicks to select an object. By comparing the drag position with the drop_start variable, CONTAIN can avoid this problem.

The second consideration is choosing if dropped objects should move into the document or simply copy themselves. Moving may not always be desirable. For example, if you drag an object from an application to one that doesn't handle as many data formats, you may lose information. To prevent this, CONTAIN moves only data inside the CONTAIN document. Data from outside sources copies by default.

All of the effect logic is in the drop_effect() function (see Listing 7-10 and CON_IF.C). The DragEnter(), DragOver(), and Drop() functions all call drop_effect(). The function first decides if the cursor is over the window's client area. If it is not, drop_effect() returns DROPEFFECT_NONE. When the cursor is over the client area, CONTAIN calls the OleStdGetDropEffect() function (an OLE2UI call). If a shift key is down, this function returns the standard interpretation for it. If no shift keys are down, the function returns zero.

Listing 7-10. The drop_effect() Function

```
/* Determine drop effect for drag and drop */
static DWORD drop_effect(POINTL p,DWORD kstate)
  {
  RECT r;
  DWORD act;
  POINT pt;
/* If shift/control down, get standard effect */
  act=OleStdGetDropEffect(kstate);
/* See if point is inside client rectangle */
  pt.x=p.x;
```

```
    pt.y=p.y;
    GetClientRect(topwindow,&r);
    ClientToScreen(topwindow,(LPPOINT)&r);
    ClientToScreen(topwindow,(LPPOINT)&r.right);
/* If cursor in non-client area or at starting point
    do nothing */
    if (!PtInRect(&r,pt)||(dragging&&p.x==drop_start.x&&
        p.y==drop_start.y))
        return DROPEFFECT_NONE;
/* If standard effect, return it */
    if (act) return act;
/* Otherwise, if local drag move else copy */
    return dragging?DROPEFFECT_MOVE:DROPEFFECT_COPY;
    }
```

When OleStdGetDropEffect() returns a non-zero value, drop_effect() returns it. Otherwise, it returns DROPEFFECT_MOVE or DROPEFFECT_COPY. If the dragging flag is set, this means the CONTAIN application is the source of the drag. The return value is then DROPEFFECT_MOVE. If dragging is clear, the drag source is another application. The drop_effect() function then returns DROPEFFECT_COPY.

With the drop_effect() function, DragEnter() and DragOver() become simple to write (see Listing 7-11). The Drop() function is only slightly more difficult. Drop() first calls drop_effect(). If the effect is DROPEFFECT_NONE, Drop() does nothing. Otherwise, it initializes some global variables (drop_data and drop_rect) and calls obj_clip() with an argument of -1. CONTAIN7 has a modified obj_clip() function that sets up some local variables and jumps into the ordinary paste routine.

Listing 7-11. Drag-and-Drop Interface Implementation

```
/* ****Drag and drop code */


/* Drag & Drop variables */
LPDATAOBJECT drop_data;      // dropped object
RECT drop_rect;              // dropped rectangle
int drop_local;              // local drop flag
POINT drop_start;            // starting location


static DWORD drop_effect(POINTL p,DWORD kstate);


/* ****IDropTarget Functions (see below for
    IDropTarget's IUnknown functions */
/* IDropTarget::DragEnter() -- return drop_effect() */
STDMETHODIMP DropTarget_DragEnter(LPDROPTARGET this,
                                  LPDATAOBJECT data,
                                  DWORD kstate, POINTL pt,
                                  LPDWORD effect)
  {
  *effect=drop_effect(pt,kstate);
  return NOERROR;
  }


/* IDropTarget::DragOver() -- return drop_effect() */
STDMETHODIMP DropTarget_DragOver(LPDROPTARGET this,
                                 DWORD kstate,POINTL pt,
                                 LPDWORD effect)
  {
  *effect=drop_effect(pt,kstate);
  return NOERROR;
  }
```

```
/* IDropTarget::DragLeave() -- ignore */
STDMETHODIMP DropTarget_DragLeave(LPDROPTARGET this)
  {
  return NOERROR;
  }


/* IDropTarget::Drop() -- do drop action */
STDMETHODIMP DropTarget_Drop(LPDROPTARGET this,
                             LPDATAOBJECT data,
                             DWORD kstate, POINTL pt,
                             LPDWORD effect)
  {
  POINT p;
/* find effect; if none, quit */
  *effect=drop_effect(pt,kstate);
  if (*effect==DROPEFFECT_NONE) return NOERROR;
/* Set up data */
  drop_data=data;
  AddRef(data);
/* Convert location to our coordinates and save */
  p.x=pt.x;
  p.y=pt.y;
  ScreenToClient(topwindow,&p);
  drop_rect.top=p.y;
  drop_rect.left=p.x;
  drop_rect.bottom=p.y+100;
  drop_rect.right=p.x+100;
/* Call clipboard code with -1 command */
  obj_clip(-1);
/* If our drag code started this, this flag tells it
   that we were the target */
  drop_local=1;
```

```
  return NOERROR;
  }


/* ****Drop Source functions */


/* IDropSource::QueryContinueDrag()
   Decide if drag should continue, cancel, or drop */
STDMETHODIMP DropSource_QueryContinueDrag(
                LPDROPSOURCE this,
                BOOL esc,
                DWORD kstate)
  {
/* If button is up, DROP! */
  if (!(kstate&MK_LBUTTON))
    return ResultFromScode(DRAGDROP_S_DROP);
/* Cancel if escape pressed or continue */
  return ResultFromScode(esc?DRAGDROP_S_CANCEL:S_OK);
  }


/* IDropSource::GiveFeedback() -- punt to OLE */
STDMETHODIMP DropSource_GiveFeedback(LPDROPSOURCE this,
                                     DWORD effect)
  {
  return ResultFromScode(DRAGDROP_S_USEDEFAULTCURSORS);
  }



/* **** IDropTarget's IUnknown functions */
/* IDropTarget::QueryInterface() */
STDMETHODIMP dt_QueryInterface(LPVOID this,
                               REFIID iid,
                               LPVOID FAR* new)
    {
```

```
    if (IsEqualIID(iid,&IID_IDropTarget))
      {
      *new=&drop_target;
      return NOERROR;
      }
    return ResultFromScode(E_NOINTERFACE);
    }


/* IDropTarget::AddRef() -- ignore (see text) */
STDMETHODIMP_(ULONG) dt_AddRef(LPVOID this)
   {
   return 1;
   }


/* IDropTarget::Release() -- ignore (see text) */
STDMETHODIMP_(ULONG) dt_Release(LPVOID this)
   {
   return 1;
   }
```

In retrospect, it would have been better to write a separate function to insert data objects because this would make the implementation much cleaner. However, when you are modifying existing code, it's sometimes easier to take the same approach that CONTAIN does.

The IDropSource interface functions (see Listing 7-11) are trivial. If your application uses the left mouse button for dragging, you probably can paste them directly into your application.

The IDropTarget interface is somewhat unusual. Since it consumes no resources and lives as long as the application does, it has no real code for AddRef() and Release(). Its QueryInterface() function is also simplistic.

Don't make the mistake of trying to return E_NOINTERFACE in all cases from a simple QueryInterface() call. In certain situations, OLE may provide surrogate objects for those you supply. Therefore, functions like RegisterDragDrop() must determine if their arguments are truly the type they should be, or if they are a surrogate. If you always return E_NOINTERFACE, OLE will decide you passed an incorrect pointer and report an error.

Other Container Features

CONTAIN is a no-frills container application. By following its model, you can build your own containers quite quickly. Once you have mastered the subtleties of OLE objects, you can progress to the more advanced features that OLE 2.0 provides for containers.

One of the most exciting additions to OLE 2.0 is in-place activation, which allows you to activate objects directly in your container window. The object's server takes over most of your menus, toolbars, and other user-interface components. Of course, the server must also support in-place activation. If either the server or the container does not support in-place activation, everything works as usual—the server opens its own window to handle the object.

Unfortunately, in-place activation is complex to implement and manage. In-place containers must support three interfaces (IOleInPlaceFrame, IOleInPlaceSite, and IOleInPlaceUI-Window). Details of menu sharing, toolbar use, accelerators, and mouse input must be carefully negotiated with the server.

Although implementing in-place activation is intimidating, don't hesitate to try it if you need it. If you start with a working container, you can probably get an in-place version operating with little difficulty.

Writing Your Own Container

When you write your own container or add container functionality to an existing application, you should follow similar steps to those in this chapter:

1. Get the application working first. You should be finished with the basic program before attempting to add OLE support.

2. Support structured storage.

3. Add the Insert Object command and draw objects.

4. Save and load objects to files.

5. Add support for multiple verbs.

6. Handle basic clipboard operations.

7. Support linking.

8. Add the Paste Special command.

9. Proceed to drag and drop and in-place activation, if desired.

By following these steps, you can reduce your OLE development to a few easily managed steps. You can get each step's code working before proceeding to the next stage (see the box entitled "Container Debugging Tips" for some advice on getting your code to work).

CONTAINER doesn't do as much error checking as a real application should. You should use the SUCCEEDED() macro after most OLE calls. If you know the function can return only S_OK or fail, you can check for that; note, however, that SUCCEEDED() is safer.

Container Debugging Tips

As you implement your own OLE containers, here are some common pitfalls and general advice:

- Be careful to return correct values from each interface function. For example, if you forget to explicitly return from a function, the caller will receive a random return value. If this value is positive, the caller may interpret the value as a successful return code, or it may fail unexpectedly.

- The OLE SDK contains an IDataObject viewer that can examine data objects you place on the clipboard (DOBJVIEW.EXE). If you are having trouble pasting your objects into other containers, this application may shed some light on the problem.

- Be sure to test your container with all the possible combinations. Your container should handle embedding and linking from files or the clipboard. You should be able to paste static items and create new OLE objects. Finally, test each case with an OLE 1.0 server and an OLE 2.0 server.

- Check out the SR2TEST program that the OLE 2.0 SDK provides. You can use this server to provide OLE 2.0 objects. Unlike an ordinary server, SR2TEST has several options that can help you debug a client. SR2TEST also lets you simulate errors for testing purposes.

- Another useful program from the OLE 2.0 SDK is LRPCSPY, which monitors the messages OLE sends between client and server. By examining the dump from LRPCSPY, you can often pinpoint where things are going wrong.

During CONTAIN's development, the first bug was quite
a stumbling block. Starting with CONTAIN2, the return
was accidentally left off the QueryInterface() function.
The return value was always the result of the final
AddRef() in that function. Most functions that called
QueryInterface() checked only the topmost bit of the
return value, which was always zero. Everything seemed
to work. In CONTAIN4, the menu_setup() function calls
OleGetClipboard(), which usually returns S_OK, failed.
Since QueryInterface() was returning a small positive
number (5, in this case), that value was propagated to the
OleGetClipboard() result.

When menu_setup() compared the result to S_OK, it
decided that no clipboard data was available. It was very
difficult to realize that a return value of 5 from
OleGetClipboard() was due to an error in a function that
seemed to work perfectly in other situations.

What happens when you detect an error depends on your
application. Be sure to release any interface pointers you are
holding before you exit a function so that you can abort your
processing after displaying an appropriate error message.

Unlike CONTAIN, your application probably supports some
private data formats. You should build these into your
IDataObject. Your container will need to support your formats
during menu initialization and for the various clipboard
commands. When pasting data, you should usually try to
paste your descriptive formats first, followed by OLE formats,
and finally any general formats you may have.

You might prefer to leave your private format code alone. You
are free to do so, but you will forfeit drag-and-drop support

for those formats. With cut and paste, you can elect to work directly with the clipboard; with drag-and-drop you must use data objects.

Summary

By making the best use of the OLE libraries (including OLE2UI), CONTAIN implements an OLE container application with a minimum of code. Your container need not be complex. By following the checklist above and making full use of the libraries, you can easily write new OLE applications or upgrade your existing code.

8

OLE Servers

WHAT'S IN THIS CHAPTER

This chapter shows how to write simple OLE servers.

PREREQUISITES

Understanding of Windows programming and OLE. You should have the OLE 2.01 SDK Documentation.

In most ways—particularly in the user interface code—servers are simpler to implement than clients. On the other hand, servers require many more interface functions, and OLE2UI provides little support. Also, because servers don't lend themselves to staged development, you have to do most of the work before you can test your server.

Still, with care, you can write your own servers. In this chapter, you'll examine a server program that you can use as a model for your own servers.

Server Basics

In Chapter 7, the CONTAIN application made extensive use of the IOleObject interface, which is the key interface that server objects provide. Server objects also implement IDataObject and IPersistStorage interfaces. In addition, the server must supply a separate IClassFactory interface. OLE calls this interface to create new instances of the server object.

Many server programs may be run as stand-alone applications. When OLE runs a program as a server, it places /Embedding (or -Embedding) as the first argument on the command line. This is the application's cue to activate its OLE-specific code.

Object Handlers

A typical OLE server application contains two parts: the application EXE file and an object handler DLL. This DLL provides surrogate OLE objects that clients can use to do limited operations on the server data when the server is not running. This greatly improves performance since the client doesn't have to start your server for every operation.

Luckily, the OLE2.DLL serves as an object handler that is adequate for most servers (see the box entitled "What's an

What's an Object Handler?

The object handler DLL (usually OLE2.DLL) allows containers to do simple operations on an object without starting a server. Since the DLL runs in the client's address space, the process can be very efficient.

The handler actually provides the container's view to all of the server interfaces. If the server is running, the handler passes the call to the server using LRPC (light remote procedure calls). In object-oriented terms, the handler **delegates** the call to the server. If the server is not running, the handler tries to satisfy the call itself. If it is unable to handle the request, it starts the server and passes the call to it.

The handler's IOleObject interface always runs the server when the client calls the DoVerb() or Update() functions. All other functions have a default action and do not start the server (some return OLE_E_NOTRUNNING).

OLE's default IDataObject interface attempts to satisfy GetData() and GetDataHere() from the object's cache. When the data is not in the cache, the handler starts the server and delegates to it. Remember, if the server is running already, the handler delegates all calls to it.

In some specialized case, you might want to write your own object handler. For example, a custom handler might know how to convert data in the cache to other supported formats. This would improve your total server performance. Still, for most developers, the extra benefit is not worth the added complexity.

Object Handler?"). Of course, if you want better performance, you can write your own object handlers or even put your entire server in a DLL, if you like. When a client uses an EXE server, OLE uses a private form of interprocess communications to communicate with it. With DLLs, the client simply makes fast, efficient function calls. Still, most servers can just use the default OLE2.DLL handler.

CLSIDs

Every server has a unique class ID (CLSID). The OLE toolkit program, UUIDGEN.EXE, can generate these IDs if you have a network card in your PC (it uses the unique network card ID). This program is unlikely to generate the same CLSID for two developers. If you don't have a network card, or you want to be absolutely sure you don't conflict, you can request a block of CLSIDs from Microsoft for your exclusive use.

For development purposes, you can use any CLSID that isn't already in use on your system. Be sure to use a unique CLSID before you ship your application, however. You can view the CLSIDs in use on your system by running the REGEDIT program with the /V option (see Chapter 6).

The Registration Database

OLE stores information about servers in the registration database (see Chapter 6 for more about the registration database and its API). One set of entries uses the server name as a key. This provides compatibility with OLE 1.0 applications. Another set of entries use the server's CLSID as a key. These entries are where the OLE 2.0 specific information resides.

Under OLE 1.0, programmers needed to make heavy use of the registration database. With OLE 2.0, you will rarely use the database directly. Your installation program can use the REGEDIT program to make the initial entries in the database. Your server should also check the database to make sure its filenames are correct. Other than that, OLE does all the database transactions for you.

Server Registration Entries

When you install your server, you must set up the registration database before OLE will recognize the application. For development purposes, you can use REGEDIT /V (see Chapter 6) to make these entries manually. You can also make REGEDIT save your entries to a file that can be reloaded later. Your installation program can use this technique to set up the database.

The REGEDIT file for PHONE (the example server in this chapter) is in Listing 8-1. You can load such a file with this simple command:

```
REGEDIT /S phone.reg
```

Listing 8-1. PHONE.REG

```
REGEDIT
HKEY_CLASSES_ROOT\PHONE = Telephone Server
HKEY_CLASSES_ROOT\PHONE\protocol\StdFileEditing\verb\1 = &Dial
HKEY_CLASSES_ROOT\PHONE\protocol\StdFileEditing\verb\0 = &Open
HKEY_CLASSES_ROOT\PHONE\protocol\StdFileEditing\server =
    phone.exe
HKEY_CLASSES_ROOT\PHONE\Insertable =
HKEY_CLASSES_ROOT\PHONE\CLSID = {00027B00-0000-0000-C000-
    000000000046}
HKEY_CLASSES_ROOT\CLSID\{00027B00-0000-0000-C000-000000000046}
    = Telephone Server
HKEY_CLASSES_ROOT\CLSID\{00027B00-0000-0000-C000-
    000000000046}\InprocHandler = OLE2.DLL
HKEY_CLASSES_ROOT\CLSID\{00027B00-0000-0000-C000-
    000000000046}\ProgID = PHONE
HKEY_CLASSES_ROOT\CLSID\{00027B00-0000-0000-C000-
    000000000046}\DefaultIcon = phone.exe 0
```

```
HKEY_CLASSES_ROOT\CLSID\{00027B00-0000-0000-C000-
   000000000046}\LocalServer = phone.exe
HKEY_CLASSES_ROOT\CLSID\{00027B00-0000-0000-C000-
   000000000046}\verb\1 = &Dial,0,2
HKEY_CLASSES_ROOT\CLSID\{00027B00-0000-0000-C000-
   000000000046}\verb\0 = &Open,0,2
HKEY_CLASSES_ROOT\CLSID\{00027B00-0000-0000-C000-
   000000000046}\Insertable =
HKEY_CLASSES_ROOT\CLSID\{00027B00-0000-0000-C000-
   000000000046}\DataFormats\GetSet\1 = 3,1,32,1
HKEY_CLASSES_ROOT\CLSID\{00027B00-0000-0000-C000-
   000000000046}\DataFormats\GetSet\0 = Embed Source,1,8,1
HKEY_CLASSES_ROOT\CLSID\{00027B00-0000-0000-C000-
   000000000046}\MiscStatus = 0
HKEY_CLASSES_ROOT\CLSID\{00027B00-0000-0000-C000-
   000000000046}\MiscStatus\1 = 1
```

Figures 8-1 and 8-2 show graphical representations of the REGEDIT entries. Note that there are two separate trees of data. The first, under the key \PHONE, is primarily for OLE 1.0 compatibility. The second, under \CLSID\{00027B00-0000-0000-C000-000000000046}, is where the OLE 2.0-specific information resides.

Here is a brief synopsis of the database entries:

- \PHONE—Service name (appears on Insert Object dialog, etc.)

- \PHONE\protocol\StdFileEditing\verb—List of verbs for OLE 1.0 clients

- \PHONE\protocol\StdFileEditing\server—Path to executable

Figure 8-1. Registration Entries for OLE 1.0 Compatibility

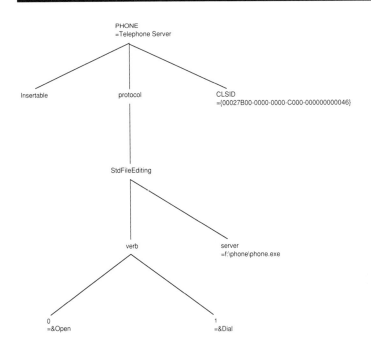

- \PHONE\protocol\StdFileEditing\Insertable—Signal to place entry in Insert Object dialog

- \PHONE\CLSID—OLE 2.0 CLSID value

- \CLSID\{000....046}—Service name (appears on Insert Object dialog, and elsewhere)

- \CLSID\{000....046}\InprocHandler—Object handler DLL (usually OLE2.DLL)

- \CLSID\{000....046}\ProgID—Program ID for OLE 1.0 database

- \CLSID\{000....046}\DefaultIcon—File and index for default icon

- \CLSID\{000....046}\LocalServer—Path to server EXE

Figure 8-2. OLE 2.0 Registration Entries

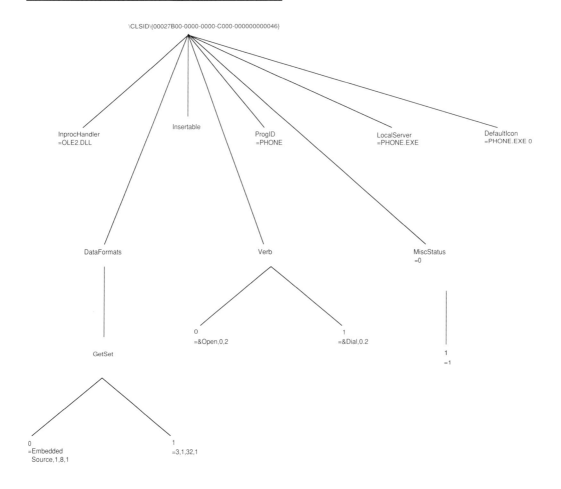

- \CLSID\{000....046}\verb—List of verbs with menu flags and options
- \CLSID\{000....046}\Insertable—Signal to make entry in Insert Object dialog
- \CLSID\{000....046}\DataFormats\GetSet—List of supported formats
- \CLSID\{000....046}\MiscStatus—Default miscellaneous status value. Subkeys are override values (see text)

Registering Verbs

Your server must register verbs in both database trees. The OLE 1.0 section lists only the verb names. In the CLSID section, the list includes two other values: options for AppendMenu() and a flag word. If bit 0 of the flag is set, the verb never modifies the object. If bit 1 is set, the verb should appear on the container's object menu. Here is an example verb entry:

```
\CLSID\{00027B00-0000-0000-C000-000000000046}\verb\1 =
    &Dial,0,2
```

This means that the Dial command is verb 1. It uses no AppendMenu() options and the container should include it on its object menu.

The MiscStatus Entry

The MiscStatus entry in the registration database allows OLE to handle the IOleObject::GetMiscStatus() call. The first value is the default status. Each subentry is the value for the specified aspect (1=DVASPECT_CONTENT, for example). The miscellaneous status bits specify important data about the object (for example, if it supports internal links or if it is static). You will read more about GetMiscStatus() later in this chapter.

Starting a Server Application

There are four steps in starting a server application:

1. Initialize the OLE libraries.

2. Update the registration database entries to reflect the location of the server.

3. Register a class factory with the OLE library. This is the interface OLE and other programs call to create an instance of the server's object.

4. Modify the server's menus and other user-interface elements to reflect that it is a server. For example, most servers change the "Exit" menu item to "Exit and Return to CONTAIN"—substituting the container's actual name, of course.

Steps 2 and 3 occur only if the server's command line contains /Embedded or -Embedded. CONTAIN calls the OLE2UI ParseCmdLine() function to detect this switch. This function also places any file name argument in a variable you supply.

The IClassFactory Interface

Table 8-1 shows the IClassFactory interface. OLE uses this interface to request new server objects from your application. The CreateInstance() function takes a CLSID as an argument and returns a new server object via a pointer argument.

Table 8-1. IClassFactory Interface

Function	Implement	Description
CreateInstance	Yes	Creates new object instance
LockServer	Optional	Prevents server from closing

The LockServer() function is optional. Some containers may lock the server when creating multiple objects. This prevents OLE from having to load the server repeatedly. Instead, the server remains running until unlocked. If you don't implement LockServer(), everything will still work, but it won't be as efficient in some cases. However, LockServer() is simple to implement. You might as well write it, although many clients don't use it.

The IPersistStorage Interface

Server objects also need to implement the IPersistStorage interface (see Table 8-2). There are only two functions (Load() and Save()) that require any real implementation. These functions simply read and write data to streams.

Table 8-2. IPersistStorage Interface

Function	Implement	Description
IsDirty	Stub	Is container's data in sync?
InitNew	Stub	Initializes new object
Load	Yes	Loads object from storage
Save	Yes	Saves object to storage
SaveCompleted	Stub	Container's save complete
HandsOffStorage	Stub	Server should not modify storage

The IDataObject Interface

The data object interface is the same one clients implement for clipboard transfers (see Chapter 7). The server's implementation needs a few more functions fleshed out, but it still does not require a complete data object (see Table 8-3). Also, OLE will automatically handle the EnumFormatEtc() function and the three advise functions, if asked.

The advise functions are necessary for server objects. Luckily, OLE handles these three functions for you. You need to inform OLE only when you want to send advisory notifications. You'll see how that works in the example server later in this chapter.

Table 8-3. The IDataObject Interface for Basic Servers

Function	Implement	Description
GetData	Yes	Gets data in new medium
GetDataHere	Yes	Gets data in existing medium
QueryGetData	Yes	Sees if data available
GetCanonicalFormatEtc	Stub	Finds equivalent format
SetData	Stub	Sets data into object
EnumFormatEtc	Stub	Enumerates formats
DAdvise	OLE	Sets up advise loop
DUnadvise	OLE	Stops advise loop
EnumDAdvise	OLE	Lists active advise loops

When writing a server, you can provide the data object interface for your internal data structure, or you can copy data to a special structure for the transfer. The example in this chapter uses a special data structure for data transfers.

The IOleObject Interface

The IOleObject interface, with its 21 functions, is certainly intimidating. Luckily, many of these functions have trivial implementations, especially if your server does not support linking (many servers do not). Table 8-4 shows the entire interface.

OLE calls the SetHostNames() function to inform the server of the client's name and document name. Under some early versions of OLE 2.0, the library passes an OLE 2.0 client's name only during object creation. With OLE 1.0 clients, the name is available during object creation and activation.

Table 8-4. IOleObject Interface

Function	Implement	Description
SetClientSite	Yes	Stores client site pointer
GetClientSite	Yes	Returns client site pointer
SetHostNames	Yes	Modifies user interface with client and document name
Close	Yes	Shuts down server
SetMoniker	Stub	Sets moniker (linking only)
GetMoniker	Stub	Gets moniker (linking only)
InitFromData	Stub	Places data in object
GetClipboardData	Stub	Returns object data
DoVerb	Yes	Handles verbs
EnumVerbs	Stub	Lists available verbs
Update	Stub	Updates linked object
IsUpToDate	Stub	Checks linked object
GetUserClassID	Yes	Returns CLSID
GetUserType	Stub	Returns server name
SetExtent	Stub	Sets bounding rectangle
GetExtent	Yes	Returns bounding rectangle
Advise	OLE	Manages advise notifications
Unadvise	OLE	Manages advise notifications
EnumAdvise	OLE	Manages advise notifications
GetMiscStatus	Stub	Returns miscellaneous status
SetColorScheme	Stub	Negotiates color scheme

The DoVerb() function is where you get to implement actual operations on your object. The verb number passed as an argument corresponds to the verb number in the registration database.

If the client wants to shut down the server, it calls the Close() function. The processing you will need to handle Close() is similar to what happens when you process the Exit command from the File menu. You will often place the code in a separate function so that you can use it in these two places.

OLE provides support for the advise functions via the CreateOleAdviseHolder() function. This is the easiest way to support the advise functions in your server. OLE also uses the registration database to satisfy GetMiscStatus(), GetUserType(), and EnumVerbs(). Simply return OLE_S_USEREG from these functions, and OLE will do the rest.

Notifications

Most communications between containers and servers occur when the container calls one of the server's interface functions. However, the server sometimes needs to notify the container of some event. To do this, the server sends notifications to the container via the OLE advise sink or the data object advise sink. The three most common advisory messages are SendOnClose(), SendOnSave(), and SendOnDataChange().

OLE requires servers to support multiple advise sinks. Luckily, OLE's CreateOleAdviseHolder() and CreateData-AdviseHolder() functions automatically provide this support. These two functions are the easiest way to implement the advise functions in your server. You'll see exactly how this works later in this chapter.

The PHONE Server

The PHONE application is a simple telephone book application that first appeared in *Commando Windows Programming* (see the bibliography and the box entitled "About PHONE"). The original PHONE program had no OLE capability. Adding OLE 2.0 server support to it is typical of what most developers will face—modifying existing code to use OLE.

As an OLE server, PHONE is different from other servers you may use. A typical server manages a document (for example, a graphics image). Since the server embeds the entire document in the client, it doesn't make sense to support Open and Save commands.

PHONE, however, embeds a single phone number entry in the client. This entry usually comes from a phone book file. Therefore, PHONE allows you to open and save phone book files even while embedding. That way, you can select a phone number from an existing phone book. OLE is flexible enough that you can support any type of arrangement that makes sense for your application. An ordinary server would disable the Open and Save menu commands.

The new OLE portions of PHONE are in PHONEOBJ.H, PHONEOBJ.C and PHONEIF.C (see listings 8-2 to 8-4 at the end of this chapter). The changes to the existing portions of code are minimal.

PHONE supports two verbs: Open and Dial. The Dial verb should dial the current number on the telephone. For demonstration purposes, the Dial verb currently puts up a simple message box that contains the phone number.

If you want to modify PHONE to actually dial, you can find an example of phone dialing in the Microsoft Software Library (look up the keyword DIAL). If you do add dialing to PHONE, you should probably make it accessible from the main menu as well.

About PHONE

The PHONE application is a simple dialog-based phone book. The user interface code is chiefly in PHONE.C and the database code is in PHONEDB.C.

Since PHONE's user interface is a dialog, it must retrieve any changes you make by sending each edit control a WM_GETTEXT message. The commit_record() function does this and transfers the results to PHONE's database. When commit_record() finds a change, it sets PHONE's dirty flag.

The reverse operation, copying a database record to the dialog box, is disp_record(). This call takes a database record pointer as an argument. However, this argument is always the current variable. The current variable contains a pointer to the current record.

PHONE is typical of a program you might want to make an OLE server. In this chapter, PHONE becomes an OLE server with almost no changes to the existing code and no changes to the existing file format. You can find a complete description of PHONE in *Commando Windows Programming* (see the bibliography).

Starting PHONE

PHONEOBJ.C (Listing 8-3) contains the ole_init() function. This function performs three separate tasks, depending on how the main code calls it. When the phase argument is zero, ole_init() initializes OLE and parses the command line looking for /Embedded (using the OLE2UI ParseCmdLine() function). If this flag is present, ole_init() sets the embedding flag. The rest of the code depends on this flag to decide if PHONE is running in stand-alone mode.

After parsing the command line, ole_init() calls the update_regdb() function. You probably can use this function in your own servers with only slight modifications. It forces the registration database to reflect the current location of the server EXE file. Of course, you'll need to modify the PHONE and myCLSIDstr strings to match your server's base name and CLSID. The function uses GetModuleFileName() to learn the EXE file's location.

PHONE calls ole_init() again after it creates its main window. This time, the phase argument is equal to 1. If the embedding flag is set, ole_init() uses the CoRegisterClassObject() call to register its class factory object with the OLE library. For a single-window server like PHONE, you need to use the REGCLS_SINGLEUSE flag with this call. This flag informs OLE that each copy of PHONE can handle one embedding. Multiple-document servers may use REGCLS_MULTIPLEUSE instead.

Finally, the main application calls ole_init() with a phase argument of 2 before shutting down. This disconnects and frees the class factory and terminates the OLE library.

By placing all the OLE-specific code in this one function, the changes to PHONE.C (the main module) are minimal. A few calls to ole_init() are all that is necessary to start and close the application. Other modifications to the original program follow a similar pattern—insert a single function call in the original and do the work in an OLE-specific source module.

The Class Factory

The PHONE server object uses the PHONEOBJ structure to hold its data (see Listing 8-2). Table 8-5 shows a synopsis of the fields in this structure. The first six fields duplicate the data in the actual phone book entry. The remaining fields provide the three required interfaces, store the reference count, the container's IOleClientSite pointer, and the OLE-provided advise holders.

The IClassFactory implementation uses the CLASSFAC structure for its own data (see Table 8-6). In addition to the usual object fields, CLASSFAC also stores a registration value (co_reg) and two flags. One flag (locked) shows the server's lock status. The other flag (made1) is set when the factory has already made one object.

Table 8-5. The PHONEOBJ Structure

Field	Description
name	Name
co	Company name
num	Phone number
fax	Fax number
email	E-mail address
notes	Comments
refct	Reference count
advisor	IDataObject advise delegate
oadvisor	IOleObject advise delegate
do_interface	IDataObject interface
ps_interface	IPersistStorage interface
oo_interface	IOleObject interface
site	Client site

Table 8-6. The CLASSFAC Structure

Field	Description
refct	Reference count
co_reg	CORegisterClassObject return value
locked	Server locked flag
made1	Flag set when one object created
cf_interface	IClassFactory interface

When the class factory processes the LockServer() function, it sets or resets the lock flag in the CLASSFAC structure. The Release() function will not free the object as long as the lock flag is set (see cfac_Release() in Listing 8-3). You may also call the OLE CoLockExternal() function to handle LockServer().

The heart of the class factory is the CreateInstance() function. If the function decides that it can satisfy the request, it allocates a PHONEOBJ structure, initializes it, and returns an interface pointer. The requested interface may be IUnknown. Since PHONE's QueryInterface() doesn't return anything for IUnknown, CreateInstance() returns the IOleObject interface in that case.

CreateInstance() fails if you try to make more than one object (the made1 flag is set) or when you attempt to aggregate a PHONE object with other OLE objects. Aggregation is a method of creating new objects from several existing objects. Since this is not necessary for ordinary OLE operations, the PHONE class factory does not allow it.

CreateInstance() can determine when OLE attempts aggregation by examining the unk field. It is ordinarily NULL. When forming an aggregate, the field will contain an IUnknown pointer. If you want to know more about aggregation, consult the OLE documentation.

Before CreateInstance() returns, it calls the new object's QueryInterface() function, which allows the object to provide the requested type of interface. It also calls AddRef() on the new object.

Providing the Server Interfaces

The three server interfaces (IPersistStorage, IDataObject, and IOleObject) are in PHONEIF.C. Although there are many functions, most have very simple implementations.

The IPersistStorage Interface

The IPersistStorage interface is the simplest of the three server interfaces. Only two functions have any real code.

The Load() function takes an IStorage pointer and reads the PHONEOBJ data from the PHONE stream in that storage. PHONE only stores the first six fields of the PHONEOBJ in the stream—CreateInstance() initializes the remaining fields when it creates the object. After the data is in the PHONEOBJ, Load() calls copy_over() to replace the data in the current telephone book record. Of course, if your data object is the application's primary data structure, you don't need to copy the data.

PHONE's Save() function is the inverse of the Load() function. It copies data from the current telephone record to the PHONEOBJ structure and writes it to the PHONE stream.

The IsDirty(), InitNew(), SaveCompleted(), and HandsOffStorage() functions require only a return. Dirty, in this context, means that the container's copy of the data is out of date with respect to the real object. Embedded objects are never dirty; only linking containers need to worry about the IsDirty() function.

The IDataObject Interface

The data object implementation for servers is very similar to the one used by containers. PHONE's data object provides a simple metafile picture that OLE can use for display purposes (see Figure 8-3). All servers must supply a metafile or bitmap so that OLE can display the object in containers.

PHONE returns OLE_S_USEREG from the EnumFormatEtc() function. This tells OLE to create a default enumerator that uses the values in the registration database, which allows you to avoid writing an enumerator object.

Figure 8-3. A PHONE Object

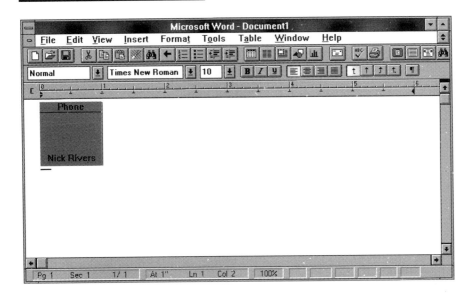

OLE handles the advise functions (DAdvise(), DUnadvise(), and EnumDAdvise()) for you. The first time PHONE processes DAdvise(), it calls CreateDataAdviseHolder(). This returns a pointer to an internal OLE object. PHONE passes on all advise calls to this internal object. When PHONE needs to send a data change notification, it calls the internal object. You'll see how PHONE handles notifications later in this chapter.

The IOleObject Interface

The IOleObject interface requires 21 functions (not counting the three IUnknown functions). While this seems daunting at first, most of them are quite simple. Like the other interfaces, many functions—eleven to be exact—are simple stubs. Many others are very simple.

The SetClientSite() and GetClientSite() functions, for example, could hardly be simpler. PHONE stores the client site pointer during SetClientSite() and returns it from GetClientSite(). The three advise functions simply use an OLE-provided OLE advise holder.

The functions that contain the most code are DoVerb(), SetHostNames(), and Close(). The DoVerb() function is as complex as your custom processing needs to be. Handling the standard SHOW and HIDE verbs is quite simple. PHONE simply activates or hides its main window and sends an OnShowWindow() notification to the container (see the next section for more on notifications).

The SetHostNames() function is not very complex. This is where PHONE learns the name of the container and the container's document. PHONE also changes and disables some menu items here.

Containers call the Close() function when they want the server to shut down. This is similar to the Exit command on the file menu, so PHONE uses the same code for each. The ole_closing() and ole_close() functions in PHONEOBJ.C do the required processing. The ole_closing() command occurs first. Then, the ole_close() command runs as part of the server's final exit code.

PHONE's Exit command always allows the user to decide if PHONE will update the container's data. You should make your decision based on your server.

The remaining functions are very simple. PHONE does not allow clients to set its object size (via the SetExtent() call). In response to a GetExtent() call, it returns a fixed, square size (2540 HIMETRIC units or 1 inch). The GetUserClassID() function simply returns the server's CLSID. The EnumVerbs(), GetUserType(), and GetMiscStatus() calls can all return OLE_S_USEREG.

Linking servers have a few more functions to flesh out. The GetMoniker() and SetMoniker() calls, for example, are necessary for link sources. Since PHONE doesn't allow linking, it can safely ignore these calls.

Sending Advisory Notifications

Basic servers must send containers four advisory messages. Two of these are via the OLE advise sink (the oadvisor field in PHONEOBJ), one is to the data object advise sink (advisor), and the other is to the IClientSite interface. Table 8-7 shows the advise functions that PHONE calls.

Table 8-7. Advise Notifications

Notification	Target	Description
SendOnSave	IOleObject	Object saved
SendOnClose	IOleObject	Server closing
OnShowWindow	IClientSite	Server window hiding or showing
SendOnDataChange	IDataObject	Object data changed

User Interface Considerations

When the PHONE server runs within a container, it should change its title and menus (see Figure 8-4). The IOleObject::SetHostNames() function does this. The title changes to

```
PHONE object in container_name
```

Also, the Exit menu item changes to

```
Exit to container_name
```

More conventional servers will also disable their Open menu commands and change Save to Update. Of course, if the server

Figure 8-4. PHONE's Main Screen

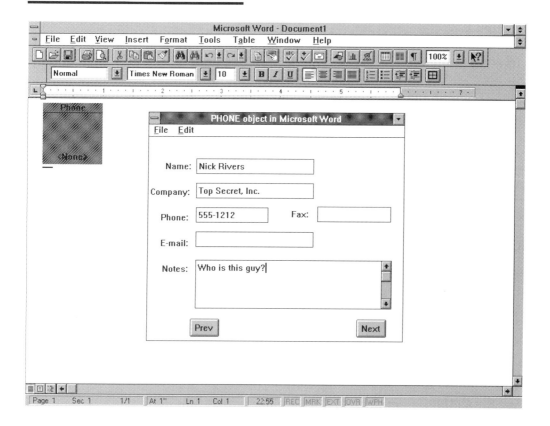

had a toolbar or other alternate methods of activating these functions, it would need to disable them as well.

Changes to Existing Code

The changes to the existing PHONE.C and PHONEDB.C are almost nonexistent. PHONE.C has several calls to ole_init() (see the preceding sections) and calls to ole_closing() and ole_close() for the Exit command. The exit processing (under WM_CLOSE) changes slightly to make the calls in the proper sequence.

PHONEDB.C calls ole_dirty() from its commit_record() function. This informs PHONE's OLE code that the user changed the data on the screen. Also, when PHONE reads a file while embedding, it sets the dirty flag.

These are the only changes in the original source code files. All other changes reside in PHONEOBJ.H, PHONEOBJ.C, and PHONEIF.C

Advanced Servers

PHONE is a simple server, not unlike some mini-servers Microsoft supplies with Word, Excel, and other products. As these mini-servers show, a server need not be sophisticated to be useful.

One simple addition you might want to make to the PHONE server is clipboard support, which would allow you to place the existing data object on the clipboard just as a container does (see Chapter 7 for more details). Making PHONE a source for drag-and-drop objects wouldn't be too hard either. However, since the main window is a dialog, you will need a creative user-interface scheme to start the drag.

A more ambitious project would be linking support. In Chapter 7, CONTAIN required a single moniker to identify the document's location. Servers must prepare multiple, complex monikers. A PHONE moniker would need to know both the phonebook file's path and the name in the phonebook. In addition, OLE requires the server to provide an absolute moniker and a relative moniker (see Chapter 7).

Linking brings up several other issues, such as updating links. Armed with what you know about basic servers and the OLE documentation, you could tackle a link source, if you needed it.

Perhaps the most ambitious servers allow in-place activation. Like in-place containers, in-place servers require a lot of negotiation for window space, menu items, toolbars, accelerators, and context-sensitive help. Still, the look and feel of an in-place server and container working together is quite flashy. Only you can balance the worth of the additional effort compared to the benefit in your application.

Writing Your Own Server

Using PHONE as a model, you can modify your existing applications to be OLE servers. You should decide early if you want to integrate the OLE interfaces with your existing data structures or use a separate OLE structure (like PHONE does).

Most of the server functionality is tied together, so you can't build in and test steps very easily. See the box entitled "Debugging Servers" for some advice on server debugging.

Summary

In many ways, OLE servers are simpler to implement than containers. This is largely because OLE provides object handler support and makes good use of the registration database.

If you want better performance from your server, you might consider writing it as a DLL (you'll need to refer to the OLE documentation for more information about doing this). DLLs are more efficient since they run in the container's address space. However, be warned: DLL servers won't work with OLE 1.0 clients, and they have trouble working with accelerators and other user interface issues. Also, if you build a 16-bit DLL server, it won't work on a 32-bit platform and vice versa. For most developers, EXE servers are more than adequate.

Debugging Servers

Since you don't run server programs directly, it is more difficult to troubleshoot and debug them. Here are a few things to look out for along with some general advice:

- You can run an ordinary debugger instead of a server. Just modify the appropriate server entry in the registration database. If you are having trouble with an OLE 1.0 client, you need to change the protocol\StdFileEditing\Server entry. Otherwise, change the LocalServer entry. In either event, the entry will look like this:

```
\....\LocalServer=c:\borlandc\bin\tdw.exe
  f:\phone\phone.exe
```

- When OLE wants to start your server, it runs the debugger (Turbo Debugger, here). The debugger then loads your server.

- Make sure that the path entries in the registration database are correct or that your server's location is in the DOS PATH variable. If your server is on the DOS PATH, make sure before shipping that your registration database update code is working properly.

- Be sure to test your server with both OLE 1.0 and 2.0 containers. Sometimes you can work with one but not the other.

- If you suspect you are having trouble with your data object, try placing it on the clipboard. You can then study it with the OLE toolkit's data object viewer (see Chapter 7 for more about this viewer).

- You may find the OLE toolkit's CL2TEST container useful as a test container. Besides being an OLE 2 container, it has some options you can use to simulate errors and view debugging information.

- The LRPCSPY program in the OLE toolkit is sometimes helpful. It monitors the messages that OLE sends between programs. By examining its output, you can often learn which OLE calls are failing.

Listing 8-2. PHONEOBJ.H

```
/* OLE-specific header for PHONE */
#define OLEFLEN 256

/* OLE Data tranfer */
typedef struct _ph_obj
  {
  char FAR name[OLEFLEN];
  char FAR co[OLEFLEN];
  char FAR num[OLEFLEN];
  char FAR fax[OLEFLEN];
  char FAR email[OLEFLEN];
  char FAR notes[OLEFLEN];
/* From here down is not saved in file */
  DWORD refct;
  /* advise holder */
  LPDATAADVISEHOLDER advisor;
  LPOLEADVISEHOLDER oadvisor;
  /* interfaces */
  struct _do_interface
    {
    IDataObjectVtbl FAR *lpVtbl;
    struct _ph_obj FAR *object;
    } do_interface;
  struct _ps_interface
    {
    IPersistStorageVtbl FAR *lpVtbl;
    struct _ph_obj FAR *object;
    } ps_interface;
  struct _oo_interface
    {
    IOleObjectVtbl FAR *lpVtbl;
```

```c
      struct _ph_obj FAR *object;
      } oo_interface;
/* Client site */
   LPOLECLIENTSITE site;
   } PHONEOBJ;

/* Class factory data */
typedef struct _cf_obj
   {
   DWORD refct;
   DWORD co_reg;
   DWORD locked;
   int made1;
   struct _cf_interface
      {
      IClassFactoryVtbl FAR *lpVtbl;
      struct _cf_obj *object;
      } cf_interface;
   } CLASSFAC;
extern CLASSFAC class_factory;
/* App running as server? */
extern int embedding;
extern IClassFactoryVtbl ph_classfactory;
extern IDataObjectVtbl do_vtbl;
extern IPersistStorageVtbl ps_vtbl;
extern IOleObjectVtbl oo_vtbl;

/* CLASS ID data */
#define myCLSIDarg 0x27B00,0,0,0xc0,0,0,0,0,0,0,0x46
#define myCLSIDstr \
   "{00027B00-0000-0000-C000-000000000046}"
extern const GUID myCLSID;
```

```
/* Prototypes */
void update_regdb(void);
int ole_init(LPSTR cmd,int phase);
void ole_save(void);
int ole_closing(void);
void ole_dirty(void);
void ole_close(void);
void err(void);
```

Listing 8-3. PHONEOBJ.C

```
/* OLE Related parts of PHONE.C */
#include <windows.h>
#define NONAMELESSUNION
#include "ole2ui.h"
#include "phone.h"
#include "phoneobj.h"
#include "..\c_ole.h"


/* Since our server only does one object,
   routines can refer to it with this
   variable */
static PHONEOBJ FAR *singleobj;

/* Define CLSID */
const GUID myCLSID=
    {
    myCLSIDarg
    };

/* Running as server? */
int embedding;
```

```
/* Class factory data */
CLASSFAC class_factory=
  {
  0,
  0,
  0,
  0,
  { &ph_classfactory, &class_factory }
  };


/* Generic function to update path entries in registration
   database */
void update_regdb()
  {
  char fn[128],*p;
  HKEY reg;
/* If you can't get the file name, give up */
  if (!GetModuleFileName(hInst,fn,sizeof(fn)))
    {
    MessageBox(NULL,"Can't find PHONE server's file name!",
      "Warning",MB_OK|MB_ICONEXCLAMATION);
    return;
    }
  if (RegOpenKey(HKEY_CLASSES_ROOT,
            "PHONE\\protocol\\StdFileEditing",
            &reg)!=ERROR_SUCCESS)
      err();
  RegSetValue(reg,"server",REG_SZ,fn,0);
  RegCloseKey(reg);
  if (RegOpenKey(HKEY_CLASSES_ROOT,
        "CLSID\\" myCLSIDstr,&reg)!=ERROR_SUCCESS)
    err();
```

```
   RegSetValue(reg,"LocalServer",REG_SZ,fn,0);
   strcat(fn," 0");
   RegSetValue(reg,"DefaultIcon",REG_SZ,fn,0);
   RegCloseKey(reg);
   }

/* DO OLE setup and shutdown */
ole_init(LPSTR cmd,int phase)
   {
   static HRESULT init;
   if (!phase)  /* Initial startup */
     {
     char filename[256];
     DWORD olever;
     SetMessageQueue(96);
     olever=OleBuildVersion();
     if (HIWORD(olever)<20)
       {
       MessageBox(NULL,
          "This application requires OLE version 2.x",
          NULL,MB_OK|MB_ICONSTOP);
       return FALSE;
       }
     init=OleInitialize(NULL);
     if (init!=S_OK) return FALSE;
/* Make sure database is correct */
     update_regdb();
/* Look for /Embedding flag */
     ParseCmdLine(cmd,&embedding,filename);
     return TRUE;
     }
   else if (phase==1)      /* Secondary startup */
```

```
    {
    if (embedding)
      {
      HRESULT r;
/* register IClassFactory object */
      if ((r=CoRegisterClassObject(&myCLSID,
          (LPUNKNOWN)&class_factory.cf_interface.lpVtbl,
          CLSCTX_LOCAL_SERVER,REGCLS_SINGLEUSE,
          &class_factory.co_reg))!=S_OK)
          {
          char dbg[33];
          wsprintf(dbg,"%lx",r);
          MessageBox(NULL,dbg,NULL,MB_OK|MB_ICONSTOP);
          return FALSE;
          }
      }
/* other server init */
    return TRUE;
    }
  else if (phase==2)    /* Shutdown */
    {
    if (init==S_OK)     /* if init was OK, undo it */
      {
      if (class_factory.co_reg)
        {
        CoDisconnectObject(
           (LPUNKNOWN)&class_factory.
             cf_interface.lpVtbl,0);
        CoRevokeClassObject(class_factory.co_reg);
        Release(((LPUNKNOWN)&class_factory.
           cf_interface.lpVtbl));
        class_factory.co_reg=0;
```

```
        }
      OleUninitialize();
        }
    }
  return FALSE;
  }


/* Convert this pointer to data structure */
#define GETOBJPTR(this)\
   (((struct _cf_interface FAR *)this)->object)



/* Class factory Query Interface */
STDMETHODIMP cfac_QueryInterface(LPVOID this,REFIID iid,
                 LPVOID FAR* new)
  {
  CLASSFAC *obj=GETOBJPTR(this);
/* Class factory interface or nothing */
  if (IsEqualIID(iid,&IID_IClassFactory))
    {
    *new=&obj->cf_interface;
    }
  else return ResultFromScode(E_NOINTERFACE);
  AddRef(((LPUNKNOWN)*new));
  return NOERROR;
  }


/* Class factory AddRef() */
STDMETHODIMP_(ULONG) cfac_AddRef(LPVOID this)
  {
  CLASSFAC *obj=GETOBJPTR(this);
  obj->refct++;
```

```
   return obj->refct;
   }


/* Class factory Release() */
STDMETHODIMP_(ULONG) cfac_Release(LPVOID this)
   {
   CLASSFAC *obj=GETOBJPTR(this);
   if (!--obj->refct) obj->made1=0;
   return obj->refct;
   }


/* IClassFactory::CreateInstance() */
STDMETHODIMP cfac_CreateInstance(LPVOID this,
                 LPUNKNOWN unk,REFIID iid,
                 LPVOID FAR *nobj)
   {
   CLASSFAC *obj=GETOBJPTR(this);
   LPMALLOC imalloc;
   PHONEOBJ FAR *p;
   HRESULT rv;
/* Only make 1 */
   if (obj->made1)
      return ResultFromScode(E_UNEXPECTED);
/* Don't allow aggregation */
   if (unk)
     return ResultFromScode(CLASS_E_NOAGGREGATION);
/* Remember that we made one */
   obj->made1=1;
/* Get IMalloc pointer and allocate
   instance of our class */
   CoGetMalloc(MEMCTX_TASK,&imalloc);
   singleobj=p=Alloc(imalloc,sizeof(PHONEOBJ));
```

```
  Release(imalloc);
  if (!p)
    return ResultFromScode(E_OUTOFMEMORY);
/* Initialize all fields */
  _fmemset(p,0,sizeof(PHONEOBJ));
/* Set up interfaces */
  p->oo_interface.object=p->ps_interface.object=
    p->do_interface.object=p;
  p->oo_interface.lpVtbl=&oo_vtbl;
  p->do_interface.lpVtbl=&do_vtbl;
  p->ps_interface.lpVtbl=&ps_vtbl;
/* return requested interface */
  if (IsEqualIID(iid,&IID_IUnknown))
    /* any one will do -- this also calls AddRef for us! */
    rv=QueryInterface(((LPUNKNOWN)&p->ps_interface),
         &IID_IOleObject,nobj);
  else
    rv=QueryInterface(((LPUNKNOWN)&p->ps_interface),
         iid,nobj);
  return rv;
  }



/* IClassFactory::LockServer() */
STDMETHODIMP cfac_LockServer(LPVOID this,BOOL lock)
  {
  CLASSFAC *obj=GETOBJPTR(this);
  obj->locked+=lock?1:-1;
  return NOERROR;
  }
```

```
/* Class Factory VTBL */
IClassFactoryVtbl ph_classfactory=
  {
  cfac_QueryInterface,
  cfac_AddRef,
  cfac_Release,
  cfac_CreateInstance,
  cfac_LockServer
  };


/* Save object */
void ole_save()
  {
  singleobj->site->lpVtbl->SaveObject(singleobj->site);
/* Advise save */
  singleobj->oadvisor->lpVtbl->
    SendOnSave(singleobj->oadvisor);
  }


/* Disable dirty processing when closing */
static int closing;

/* Get ready to close */
int ole_closing()
  {
  int rv;
  closing=1;
/* commit changes, don't clear dirty flag */
  commit_record(current);
  closing=0;
  if (dirty)
```

```
    {
    rv=MessageBox(topwindow,
        "Update container?",
        "Confirm",MB_YESNOCANCEL);
    if (rv==IDYES)
      {
      ole_dirty();
      ole_save();
      }
    }
/* Advise */
  if (rv!=IDCANCEL)
      singleobj->site->lpVtbl->
        OnShowWindow(singleobj->site,FALSE);
  return rv;
  }


/* Process when dirty */
void ole_dirty()
  {
  int i;
  if (closing) return;
/* Update OLE transfer object */
  for (i=0;i<NRFIELDS;i++)
    _fstrcpy(singleobj->name+i*OLEFLEN,
              current->fields[i]);
  dirty=0;
/* Send advise */
  if (singleobj->advisor)
    singleobj->advisor->lpVtbl->SendOnDataChange(
              singleobj->advisor,
              (LPDATAOBJECT)&singleobj->do_interface,
```

```
                         0,ADVF_NODATA);
  }


/* Final close */
void ole_close()
  {
/* Don't let object release early */
  AddRef(((LPUNKNOWN)&singleobj->do_interface));
  if (singleobj->advisor)
    {
/* Advise */
    singleobj->advisor->lpVtbl->
              SendOnDataChange(singleobj->advisor,
              (LPDATAOBJECT)&singleobj->do_interface,
              0,ADVF_DATAONSTOP);
    }
/* Advise */
  if (singleobj->oadvisor)
    {
    singleobj->oadvisor->lpVtbl->
        SendOnClose(singleobj->oadvisor);
    }
/* Hide server */
  ShowWindow(topwindow,SW_HIDE);
/* Advise window hidden */
  singleobj->site->lpVtbl->
      OnShowWindow(singleobj->site,FALSE);
/* Release our first ref */
  Release(((LPUNKNOWN)&singleobj->do_interface));
/* Ask CO to unlock object */
  CoLockObjectExternal((LPUNKNOWN)&class_factory.
        cf_interface.lpVtbl,FALSE,TRUE);
```

```
  }

/* Sketetal error handler -- need more here */
void err()
  {
  MessageBox(NULL,"Error!",NULL,MB_OK|MB_ICONSTOP);
  }
```

Listing 8-4. PHONEIF.C

```c
/* PHONE Server interface functions */
#include <windows.h>
#define NONAMELESSUNION
#include "ole2ui.h"
#include <stdlib.h>
#include "phone.h"
#include "phoneobj.h"
#include "..\c_ole.h"


/* Convert this pointer to data structure */
#define GETOBJPTR(this) (((struct _oo_interface FAR *)\
                          this)->object)



/* IUnknown interface elements */

/* Query Interface */
STDMETHODIMP po_QueryInterface(LPVOID this,REFIID iid,
                 LPVOID FAR* new)
    {
    PHONEOBJ FAR *obj=GETOBJPTR(this);
/* IOleObject? */
    if (IsEqualIID(iid, &IID_IOleObject))
```

```
            *new = &obj->oo_interface;
/* IPersist or IPersistStorage? */
    else if (IsEqualIID(iid, &IID_IPersistStorage)
            ||IsEqualIID(iid, &IID_IPersist))
        *new = &obj->ps_interface;
/* IDataObject? */
    else if (IsEqualIID(iid,&IID_IDataObject))
        *new = &obj->do_interface;
/* Say What? */
    else
        return ResultFromScode(E_NOINTERFACE);
    AddRef((*(LPUNKNOWN FAR *)new));
    return NOERROR;
    }


/* Add reference */
STDMETHODIMP_(ULONG) po_AddRef(LPVOID this)
  {
  PHONEOBJ FAR *obj=GETOBJPTR(this);
  return ++(obj->refct);
  }


/* Release -- this ends application unless
   server is locked */
STDMETHODIMP_(ULONG) po_Release(LPVOID this)
  {
  ULONG ret;
  PHONEOBJ FAR *obj=GETOBJPTR(this);
  if (!obj->refct) return 0;
  ret=--(obj->refct);
  if (!obj->refct)
    {
```

```
    LPMALLOC imalloc;
    ShowWindow(topwindow,SW_HIDE);
    Release(obj->site);
    if (obj->advisor)
      {
      Release(obj->advisor);
      obj->advisor=NULL;
      }
    if (obj->oadvisor)
      {
/* Advise closing */
      obj->oadvisor->lpVtbl->SendOnClose(obj->oadvisor);
      Release(obj->oadvisor);
      obj->oadvisor=NULL;
      }
    /* delete object here */
    CoGetMalloc(MEMCTX_TASK,&imalloc);
    Free(imalloc,obj);
    Release(imalloc);
    if (!class_factory.locked)
      {
      if (!IsWindow(maindlg)) DestroyWindow(maindlg);
      if (!IsWindow(topwindow)) DestroyWindow(topwindow);
      PostQuitMessage(0);
      }
    class_factory.made1=0;
    }
  return ret;
  }
/* **** IPersistStorage functions */

/* IPersistStorage::GetClassID() */
STDMETHODIMP ps_GetClassID(LPVOID this,LPCLSID class_id)
```

```
  {
  *class_id=myCLSID;
  return NOERROR;
  }


/* IPersistStorage::IsDirty()
   -- unless linking, this is always false */
STDMETHODIMP ps_IsDirty(LPVOID this)
  {
  return ResultFromScode(S_FALSE);
  }


/* IPersistStorage::InitNew() -- not needed */
STDMETHODIMP ps_InitNew(LPVOID this,LPSTORAGE sto)
  {
  return NOERROR;
  }


/* Helper function -- copy field from OLE transfer
   object to main structure */
static void copyover(char **fld,LPSTR new)
  {
  if (*fld) free(*fld);
  *fld=calloc(_fstrlen(new)+1,1);
  _fstrcpy(*fld,new);
  }


/* IPersistStorage::Load() -- Load from storage */
STDMETHODIMP ps_Load(LPVOID this,LPSTORAGE sto)
  {
  PHONEOBJ FAR *obj=GETOBJPTR(this);
  HRESULT rv;
```

```
  LPSTREAM data;
  int i;
  OpenStream(sto,"phone",NULL,
     STGM_READ|STGM_SHARE_EXCLUSIVE|STGM_DIRECT,
     0,&data);
/* Only read first part of structure */
  rv=Read(data,obj,OLEFLEN*NRFIELDS,NULL);
/* Copy to underlying PHONE structure */
  for (i=0;i<NRFIELDS;i++)
    copyover(&current->fields[i],obj->name+i*OLEFLEN);
/* Force display */
  disp_record(current);
  Release(data);
  return rv;
  }


/* IPersistStorage::Save() -- Save to storage */
STDMETHODIMP ps_Save(LPVOID this,LPSTORAGE sto)
  {
  PHONEOBJ FAR *obj=GETOBJPTR(this);
  HRESULT rv;
  LPSTREAM data;
  int i;
/* Copy all fields to OLE structure */
  for (i=0;i<NRFIELDS;i++)
    _fstrcpy(obj->name+i*OLEFLEN,current->fields[i]);
  CreateStream(sto,"phone",
          STGM_WRITE|STGM_SHARE_EXCLUSIVE|STGM_DIRECT|
          STGM_CREATE,NULL,NULL,&data);
  rv=Write(data,obj,OLEFLEN*NRFIELDS,NULL);
  Release(data);
  return rv;
  }
```

```
/* IPersistStorage::SaveCompleted() -- not needed */
STDMETHODIMP ps_SaveCompleted(LPSTORAGE sto)
  {
  return NOERROR;
  }


/* IPersistStorage::HandsOffStorage() -- not needed */
STDMETHODIMP ps_HandsOffStorage(LPSTORAGE sto)
  {
  return NOERROR;
  }


/* *** IDataObject functions */


/* IDataObject::GetData() */
STDMETHODIMP do_GetData(LPDATAOBJECT this,LPFORMATETC fmt,
                             LPSTGMEDIUM medium)
   {
   LPDATAOBJECT dataobj;
   PHONEOBJ FAR *obj=GETOBJPTR(this);
/* We supply metafile */
   if (CF_METAFILEPICT==fmt->cfFormat)
     {
     HDC mfdc;
     void FAR *p;
     METAFILEPICT mf;
     HANDLE memblk;
     RECT r;
/* Start memory metafile drawing */
     mfdc=CreateMetaFile(NULL);
     mf.mm=MM_ANISOTROPIC;
     SetMapMode(mfdc, MM_ANISOTROPIC);
```

```
    SetWindowOrg(mfdc,r.left=0,r.top=0);
    SetWindowExt(mfdc, r.right=2540, r.bottom=-2540);
/* Draw box */
    FillRect(mfdc,&r,GetStockObject(GRAY_BRUSH));
    SelectObject(mfdc,GetStockObject(SYSTEM_FONT));
    SelectObject(mfdc,GetStockObject(BLACK_PEN));
    SelectObject(mfdc,GetStockObject(BLACK_BRUSH));
    SetTextAlign(mfdc,TA_CENTER|TA_BOTTOM|TA_NOUPDATECP);
    SetBkMode(mfdc,TRANSPARENT);
    mf.xExt=2540;
    mf.yExt=2540;
/* Write text */
    TextOut(mfdc,1270,-400,"Phone",5);
    MoveTo(mfdc,0,-410);
    LineTo(mfdc,2540,-410);
    TextOut(mfdc,1270,-2440,*obj->name?obj->name:
            "<None>",*obj->name?_fstrlen(obj->name):6);
/* Close and get metafile handle */
    mf.hMF=CloseMetaFile(mfdc);
    memblk=GlobalAlloc(GMEM_SHARE|GMEM_ZEROINIT,
                       sizeof(mf));
/* Move metafilepict to global memory block */
    p=GlobalLock(memblk);
    hmemcpy(p,&mf,sizeof(mf));
    GlobalUnlock(memblk);
/* Set up for return */
    medium->tymed=TYMED_MFPICT;
    medium->u.hGlobal=memblk;
    medium->pUnkForRelease=NULL;
    return memblk?NOERROR:
            ResultFromScode(DATA_E_FORMATETC);
    }
```

```
/* Only metafiles please */
    return ResultFromScode(DATA_E_FORMATETC);
    }


STDMETHODIMP do_GetDataHere(LPDATAOBJECT this,
                    LPFORMATETC fmt, LPSTGMEDIUM medium)
    {
    PHONEOBJ FAR *obj=GETOBJPTR(this);
/* We will return embedded source here */
    if (RegisterClipboardFormat(CF_EMBEDSOURCE)==
         fmt->cfFormat&&
        fmt->tymed==TYMED_ISTORAGE)
        {
        LPSTREAM data;
/* Write object to caller's storage */
        medium->tymed=TYMED_ISTORAGE;
        medium->pUnkForRelease=NULL;
        CreateStream(medium->u.pstg,"phone",
                STGM_WRITE|STGM_SHARE_EXCLUSIVE|
                STGM_DIRECT|STGM_CREATE,
                NULL,NULL,&data);
        Write(data,obj,OLEFLEN*NRFIELDS,NULL);
        Release(data);
        return NOERROR;
        }
    return ResultFromScode(DATA_E_FORMATETC);
    }
/* Will getdata succeed? */
STDMETHODIMP do_QueryGetData(LPDATAOBJECT this,
                    LPFORMATETC fmt)
    {
/* We only support content */
```

```
    if (fmt->dwAspect!=DVASPECT_CONTENT)
      return ResultFromScode(DV_E_DVASPECT);
/* We can do Embedded source */
    if (fmt->cfFormat==
        RegisterClipboardFormat(CF_EMBEDSOURCE))
          return S_OK;
/* Or metafile pict */
    if (fmt->cfFormat==CF_METAFILEPICT)
      return S_OK;
/* Other than that, forget it */
    return ResultFromScode(DATA_E_FORMATETC);
    }


/* IDataObject::GetCanonicalFormatEtc()
 Get base FORMATETC -- ignore */
STDMETHODIMP do_GetCanonicalFormatEtc(LPDATAOBJECT this,
                LPFORMATETC in_fmt,LPFORMATETC out_fmt)
    {
    return ResultFromScode(DATA_S_SAMEFORMATETC);
    }
/* IDataObject::SetData() -- we don't do that */
STDMETHODIMP do_SetData(LPDATAOBJECT this,
                            LPFORMATETC fmt,
                            LPSTGMEDIUM medium,
                            BOOL flag)

  {
  return ResultFromScode(E_FAIL);
  }


/* IDataObject::EnumFormatEtc()
  Enumerate formats -- Use REG database */
STDMETHODIMP do_EnumFormatEtc(LPDATAOBJECT this,
                DWORD dir,LPENUMFORMATETC FAR *fmt)
```

```
   {
   return ResultFromScode(OLE_S_USEREG);
   }


/* IDataObject::DAdvise() -- hand off to OLE */
STDMETHODIMP do_DAdvise(LPDATAOBJECT this,
                               LPFORMATETC fmt,
                               DWORD advisef,
                               LPADVISESINK sink,
                               DWORD FAR *connect)
  {
  PHONEOBJ FAR *obj=GETOBJPTR(this);
/* Create advise holder first time */
  if (!obj->advisor)
    {
    if (CreateDataAdviseHolder(&obj->advisor)!=S_OK)
       return ResultFromScode(E_OUTOFMEMORY);
    }
  return
    Advise(obj->advisor,this,fmt,advisef,sink,connect);
  }


/* IDataObject::DUnadvise() -- delegate to OLE */
STDMETHODIMP do_DUnadvise(LPDATAOBJECT this,
                              DWORD connect)
  {
  PHONEOBJ FAR *obj=GETOBJPTR(this);
  if (!obj->advisor)
     return ResultFromScode(E_FAIL);
  return Unadvise(obj->advisor,connect);
  }
```

```
/* IDataObject::EnumDAdvise() -- delegate to OLE */
STDMETHODIMP do_EnumDAdvise(LPDATAOBJECT this,
                               LPENUMSTATDATA FAR *advise)
  {
  PHONEOBJ FAR *obj=GETOBJPTR(this);
  if (!obj->advisor)
     return ResultFromScode(E_FAIL);
  return EnumAdvise(obj->advisor,advise);
  }


/* **** IOleObject interface */
/* IOleObject::SetClientSite()
   -- Store away client site for later use */
STDMETHODIMP oo_SetClientSite(LPVOID this,
                    LPOLECLIENTSITE site)
  {
  PHONEOBJ FAR *obj=GETOBJPTR(this);
  obj->site=site;
  AddRef(site);
  return S_OK;
  }


/* IOleObject::GetClientSite()
   -- Return client site */
STDMETHODIMP oo_GetClientSite(LPVOID this,
                 LPOLECLIENTSITE FAR *site)
  {
  PHONEOBJ FAR *obj=GETOBJPTR(this);
  *site=obj->site;
  AddRef(obj->site);
  return S_OK;
  }
```

```
/* IOleObject::SetHostNames() -- Here is where client
   tells us about himself */
STDMETHODIMP oo_SetHostNames(LPVOID this,LPSTR app,
                                LPSTR obj)
  {
  char title[128];
  HMENU menu=GetMenu(topwindow);
  /* Set title */
  wsprintf(title,"PHONE object in %s",(LPSTR)app);
  SendMessage(topwindow,WM_SETTEXT,0,(DWORD)title);
  /* Set menu... */
/* PHONE doesn't disable any menus, but most servers
   will -- see text */
//  EnableMenuItem(menu,IDM_LOAD,MF_BYCOMMAND|MF_GRAYED);
//  EnableMenuItem(menu,IDM_SAVE,MF_BYCOMMAND|MF_GRAYED);
//  EnableMenuItem(menu,IDM_SAVEAS,
//                      MF_BYCOMMAND|MF_GRAYED);
/* Modify exit menu */
  wsprintf(title,"E&xit to %s",(LPSTR)app);
  ModifyMenu(menu,IDM_EXIT,
        MF_STRING|MF_BYCOMMAND,IDM_EXIT,(DWORD)title);
  return ResultFromScode(S_OK);
  }


/* IOleObject::Close() */
STDMETHODIMP oo_Close(LPVOID this,DWORD save)
  {
  PHONEOBJ FAR *obj=GETOBJPTR(this);
  if (save==OLECLOSE_PROMPTSAVE&&dirty)
    {
      switch (ole_closing())
        {
```

```
        case IDCANCEL:
          return ResultFromScode(OLE_E_PROMPTSAVECANCELLED);
        }
    }
  else if (save==OLECLOSE_SAVEIFDIRTY&&dirty)
    {
    ole_save();
    obj->oadvisor->lpVtbl->SendOnSave(obj->oadvisor);
    }
  /* Advise */
  obj->site->lpVtbl->
        OnShowWindow(obj->site,FALSE);
  SendMessage(topwindow,WM_CLOSE,0,0);
  return S_OK;
  }


/* IOleObject::SetMoniker() -- only needed for linking */
STDMETHODIMP oo_SetMoniker(LPVOID this,DWORD which,
                  LPMONIKER pmk)
  {
  return ResultFromScode(E_NOTIMPL);
  }


/* IOleObject::GetMoniker() -- only needed for linking */
STDMETHODIMP oo_GetMoniker(LPVOID this,DWORD assign,
                  DWORD which,LPMONIKER FAR *pmk)
  {
  return ResultFromScode(E_NOTIMPL);
  }


/* IOleObject::InitFromData() -- not needed */
STDMETHODIMP oo_InitFromData(LPVOID this,
```

```
                              LPDATAOBJECT dobj,BOOL create,
                              DWORD n_a)
   {
   return ResultFromScode(E_FAIL);
   }


/* IOleObject::GetClipboardData() -- not needed */
STDMETHODIMP oo_GetClipboardData(LPVOID this, DWORD n_a,
                         LPDATAOBJECT FAR *dobj)
   {
   return ResultFromScode(E_FAIL);
   }


/* IOleObject::DoVerb() -- Process verb */
STDMETHODIMP oo_DoVerb(LPVOID this, LONG verb,LPMSG msg,
               LPOLECLIENTSITE site,
               LONG lindex,HWND parent,LPCRECT r)
   {
   PHONEOBJ FAR *obj=GETOBJPTR(this);
   switch (verb)
     {
     case OLEIVERB_PRIMARY:
     case OLEIVERB_OPEN:
     case OLEIVERB_SHOW:
       ShowWindow(topwindow,SW_SHOWNORMAL);
       SetFocus(topwindow);
       obj->site->lpVtbl->OnShowWindow(obj->site,TRUE);
       break;

     case OLEIVERB_HIDE:
       ShowWindow(topwindow,SW_HIDE);
       obj->site->lpVtbl->OnShowWindow(obj->site,FALSE);
       break;
```

```
    case 1:         // Dial
        MessageBox(topwindow,obj->num,"Dialing...",MB_OK);
/* Close server after dialing. Don't use SendMessage --
    Give OLE time to return and finish */
        PostMessage(topwindow,WM_CLOSE,0,0);
        break;

    default:
        return ResultFromScode(OLEOBJ_S_INVALIDVERB);
    }
    return NOERROR;
    }
/* IOleObject::EnumVerbs() -- use Reg database */
STDMETHODIMP oo_EnumVerbs(LPVOID this,
                    LPENUMOLEVERB FAR *venum)
    {
    return ResultFromScode(OLE_S_USEREG);
    }


/* IOleObject::Update() -- Not needed */
STDMETHODIMP oo_Update(LPVOID this)
    {
    return NOERROR;
    }


/* IOleObject::IsUpToDate() -- Always true
    for embedded object */
STDMETHODIMP oo_IsUpToDate(LPVOID this)
    {
    return NOERROR;
    }
```

```
/* IOleObject::GetUserClassID() -- Return CLSID */
STDMETHODIMP oo_GetUserClassID(LPVOID this,CLSID FAR *id)
    {
    *id=myCLSID;
    return NOERROR;
    }
/* IOleObject::GetUserType() -- Return string name
    of object (use registration database */
STDMETHODIMP oo_GetUserType(LPVOID this,LPSTR FAR *type)
    {
    return ResultFromScode(OLE_S_USEREG);
    }


/* IOleObject::SetExtent() -- Set object size
    PHONE ignores this */
STDMETHODIMP oo_SetExtent(LPVOID this,DWORD aspect,
                LPSIZEL size)
    {
    return ResultFromScode(E_FAIL);
    }


/* IOleObject::GetExtent() -- Return object size */
STDMETHODIMP oo_GetExtent(LPVOID this,DWORD aspect,
                LPSIZEL size)
    {
/* 25.4 mm (1 inch) */
    size->cx=2540;
    size->cy=2540;
    return S_OK;
    }


/* IOleObject::Advise() -- delegate to OLE */
```

```
STDMETHODIMP oo_Advise(LPVOID this,LPADVISESINK sink,
                DWORD FAR *connect)
    {
    PHONEOBJ FAR *obj=GETOBJPTR(this);
/* Make advise holder on first call */
    if (!obj->oadvisor)
      CreateOleAdviseHolder(&obj->oadvisor);
#undef Advise
    return obj->oadvisor->lpVtbl->
          Advise(obj->oadvisor,sink,connect);
    }


/* IOleObject::Unadvise()
    delegate to OLE */
STDMETHODIMP oo_Unadvise(LPVOID this,DWORD connect)
    {
    PHONEOBJ FAR *obj=GETOBJPTR(this);
    return Unadvise(obj->oadvisor,connect);
    }


/* IOleObject::EnumAdvise()
    Delegate to OLE */
STDMETHODIMP oo_EnumAdvise(LPVOID this,
                LPENUMSTATDATA FAR *enums)
    {
    PHONEOBJ FAR *obj=GETOBJPTR(this);
    return EnumAdvise(obj->oadvisor,enums);
    }


/* IOleObject::GetMiscStatus()
    Use registration database */
```

```
STDMETHODIMP oo_GetMiscStatus(LPVOID this,
                 DWORD aspect,DWORD FAR *status)
   {
   return ResultFromScode(OLE_S_USEREG);
   }


/* IOleObject::SetColorScheme() -- ignore */
STDMETHODIMP oo_SetColorScheme(LPVOID this,
             LPLOGPALETTE pal)
   {
   return ResultFromScode(E_NOTIMPL);
   }


/* VTBLs */
IDataObjectVtbl do_vtbl=
   {
   po_QueryInterface,
   po_AddRef,
   po_Release,
   do_GetData,
   do_GetDataHere,
   do_QueryGetData,
   do_GetCanonicalFormatEtc,
   do_SetData,
   do_EnumFormatEtc,
   do_DAdvise,
   do_DUnadvise,
   do_EnumDAdvise
   };


IPersistStorageVtbl ps_vtbl=
   {
```

```
    po_QueryInterface,
    po_AddRef,
    po_Release,
    ps_GetClassID,
    ps_IsDirty,
    ps_InitNew,
    ps_Load,
    ps_Save,
    ps_SaveCompleted,
    ps_HandsOffStorage
    };

IOleObjectVtbl oo_vtbl=
    {
    po_QueryInterface,
    po_AddRef,
    po_Release,
    oo_SetClientSite,
    oo_GetClientSite,
    oo_SetHostNames,
    oo_Close,
    oo_SetMoniker,
    oo_GetMoniker,
    oo_InitFromData,
    oo_GetClipboardData,
    oo_DoVerb,
    oo_EnumVerbs,
    oo_Update,
    oo_IsUpToDate,
    oo_GetUserClassID,
    oo_GetUserType,
    oo_SetExtent,
```

```
oo_GetExtent,
oo_Advise,
oo_Unadvise,
oo_EnumAdvise,
oo_GetMiscStatus,
oo_SetColorScheme
};
```

9

OLE and IPC Wrap Up

WHAT'S IN THIS CHAPTER

As you implement your own OLE and DDE software, you may find the advice in this chapter useful.

PREREQUISITES

Basic understanding of the preceding chapters.

Windows supports three rich forms of IPC: the clipboard, DDE, and OLE. Of these, OLE is the method with a future. Of course, the clipboard will always be around for users, but from a programmer's point of view, using OLE data objects for all clipboard transactions in new software is a good idea.

Microsoft is trying to move programmers toward OLE and away from DDE. While this is largely a good thing, many programmers still need to support DDE. For example, real-time data acquisition is usually too demanding for the current implementation of OLE. Even so, OLE is certainly here to stay and you should give serious consideration to adding OLE support to your software, if it is appropriate.

More OLE

This book has only scratched the surface of OLE programming for interprocess communications. Here are some important ideas you may want to research on your own:

- You can use the IDataObject interface to represent any data you need to transfer between programs or between parts of your own programs.

- The structured storage system contains sophisticated transaction processing features. In addition to their traditional database and online transaction processing uses, these features can simplify implementing undo in your applications.

- OLE supports automation, which allows you to expose a set of functions to other programs. Other programs can then call these functions to make your program perform the specified action. Soon, sophisticated macro and batch languages will be able to have complete control of applications that support OLE automation. You might even use automation within your own application to provide customizable menus and toolbars.

- The OLE object system can provide any number of features. For example, an OLE file open object might one day replace the current common dialog function. You can easily extend the Windows system by providing OLE objects that perform services.

- The simplified methods for writing OLE clients and servers may not be the most efficient way to do things. Custom processing of the advise functions and custom object handlers, for example, can improve performance dramatically. Only you can decide if the potential gain in performance warrants the additional effort. Of course, you should always get your program working without these extras first—if you decide you need them, you can always add them.

Using C++

Although the examples in this book are in C, OLE naturally adapts to C++. With C++, your interface implementations are somewhat cleaner—the ubiquitous this pointer is automatic in C++, for example. Still, C++ objects do not directly map to OLE objects. OLE uses a different system of construction, destruction, and inheritance. You can't just drop C++ objects in as OLE objects.

The basic strategy for implementing C++ OLE objects is about the same as C. You can omit the this pointer in all the interface functions—the C++ compiler automatically includes it. You can also omit the annoying lpVtbl's scattered everywhere. You will find several C++ examples in the OLE documentation.

You might wonder why Microsoft didn't just directly use C++ for OLE. The answer is compatibility. OLE objects represent a common language for Windows applications. Thus, you can implement an object in C++ that another programmer uses in BASIC. In the future, you can expect many languages and language-like systems to support OLE objects.

Using Class Libraries

C++ class libraries exist that assist developers in using OLE (the Microsoft Foundation Classes, for example). Of course, these libraries require you to adopt their Windows application style completely—you can't selectively add them to existing applications.

The Microsoft Foundation Class (MFC) library, for example, requires you to create C++ objects that represent your application, its documents, and the views of the document. Once you organize your program in this way, MFC makes many operations simple, including OLE support.

The downside to these class libraries is that you must abandon conventional Windows programming practices. If you are starting from scratch, know C++, and dislike the conventional approach to Windows programming, these class libraries may be a good choice for you. If you don't know C++, have an existing application, or don't want to retrain for a new approach to doing things, you will probably want to avoid these libraries.

How easy is OLE support under MFC? Very easy. Figure 9-1 shows the AppWizard dialog box you use to create MFC applications. Simply checking the OLE box makes your program an OLE client. Of course, you still have to add your specific code, which will look very different from ordinary windows code (for more about MFC, see *Commando Windows Programming* in the bibliography).

Figure 9-1. MFC's Application Wizard

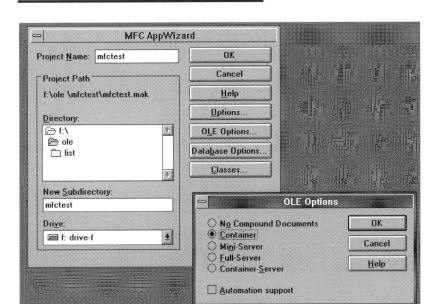

As this is written, Borland's OWL framework does not support OLE 2.0, but it probably will soon. Until then, Borland OWL programmers, or anyone else who wants to write OLE programs without MFC, will need to use more conventional techniques.

Future Versions of Windows

Although OLE 2.0 is an add-on feature of Windows 3.1, future versions of Windows (such as the upcoming Chicago) are likely to support it directly. It isn't hard to imagine the day that Windows will supply the entire API via objects. There will probably still be a function call compatibility layer, but the native calls will be to objects.

It is probable that in-place activation of objects will one day create a new class of application. Sophisticated container applications will play host to a variety of objects, integrating them as a whole document. These containers will do nothing by themselves—they will be a blank canvas for you to fill as you desire.

OLE allows in-place objects to use two different styles of activation. The most common method is similar to ordinary object activation. The user double-clicks the object, and its server opens (in place, of course). However, objects can also be always active. In this situation, it is not clear to the user that the object is separate from the current application.

Perhaps one day, you will create applications by dragging objects from a palette to a programming container (not unlike designing a dialog or a Visual Basic form). Your palette's tools could include a Microsoft Word document area, a 24-bit image editor, or a sound recorder with compression. When you were satisfied with your work, you would save your program and distribute it to end users.

OLE on Multiple Platforms

Future versions of OLE will work across network boundaries. This opens the door to Windows applications embedding documents from Macintosh computers, UNIX machines, or workstations. Thanks to OLE's object handler architecture, programmers shouldn't have to worry too much about machine details (such as byte ordering and word size).

Still, it is a good idea to think about portability when designing OLE data structures. For example, avoid using the int data type since it has different sizes on different machines. Instead use short, long, or any of the Windows integer types (DWORD or ULONG, for example).

Summary

OLE is more than a new set of APIs for Windows. It represents the first step in Windows' evolution to an object-oriented operating system. Future applications will use objects and in-place activation the way current applications use DLLs and child window controls.

Although the OLE universe is bold new territory, it is still accessible to any Windows programmer using conventional tools and techniques. Getting your applications ready for OLE today will give you a head start on the future.

Appendix
OLE 2 and Borland
C/C++

Although the OLE 2 toolkit works best with Microsoft Visual C++, you can get it to work with Borland C with just a little effort. There are three major problem areas:

- Nameless unions
- Long identifiers
- The OLE2UI makefile

Each of these problems has simple solutions. Armed with the information in this appendix, you should have no difficulty using the OLE SDK with Borland C.

Nameless Unions

The Microsoft compiler allows a common extension to ANSI C, nameless unions. Suppose you have the following structure:

```
struct abc
    {
    int type;
    union
        {
        char *p;
        float val;
        } v;
    }#a_abc;
```

Each time you wish to reference a value in the union, you must use the v as in

```
p1=a_abc.v.p;
```

If the field names of the union are unique with respect to the other fields in the structure, the v is somewhat superfluous. Therefore, some compilers allow you to omit the v from the structure definition or the reference. Then you could write

```
p1=a_abc.p;
```

Since Visual C++ allows this, the OLE headers make use of nameless unions, which upsets the Borland compiler. However, if you define the NONAMELESSUNION macro, the OLE headers add union tags to all union definitions. Simply place the following line in your source before you include any OLE headers:

```
#define NONAMELESSUNION
```

Alternatively, you can use the -DNONAMELESSUNION option on the command line.

It is a good idea to do this to your code even if you are using a compiler that supports nameless unions. If you avoid nameless unions in your code, it will be more ANSI compliant and, thus, more portable. The code in this book, for example, never uses nameless unions. This allows the programs to compile under Microsoft or Borland C.

Long Identifiers

The OLE2UI library has at least one function name that is too long for the Borland C compiler's symbol table. This call is OleStdGetObjectDescriptorDataFromOleObject() (you might be tempted to argue that this name is too long period). The Borland compiler does not mind the long symbol name, but it truncates it in the OBJ file to OleStdGetObjectDescriptorDataFro.

If you are using a version of OLE2UI compiled with Microsoft C (for example, if you are practicing with OUTLUI.DLL), you need to add the following statement to your application's .DEF file:

```
IMPORTS
  OLESTDGETOBJECTDESCRIPTORDATAFRO=
    OUTLUI.OLESTDGETOBJECTDESCRIPTORDATAFROMOLEOBJECT
```

This will successfully translate the short Borland name to the longer Microsoft name.

On the other hand, if you are using a DLL compiled with Borland C (like the AWOLEUI.DLL file in this book) and writing with Microsoft C, you need this statement in the .DEF file:

```
IMPORTS
  OLESTDGETOBJECTDESCRIPTORDATAFROMOLEOBJECT=
    AWOLEUI.OLESTDGETOBJECTDESCRIPTORDATAFRO
```

This simply reverses the transformation, allowing the Microsoft linker to find the shorter name in the Borland import library. Of course, in both cases you need to use the appropriate DLL name instead of OUTLUI or AWOLEUI.

The OLE2UI makefile

The OLE2UI makefile that comes with the OLE SDK is for Visual C++. However, you can modify it to work with Borland C. The following is a list of changes that will change MAKEDLL to work with the Borland compiler. You can make similar changes to the static makefile, if you wish.

Add these lines near the top, substituting the correct path-names for your system:

```
INCDIR=f:\ole21\include
STDINCDIR=f:\bc4\include;$(INCDIR)
```

Change these definitions:

```
CC=bcc
RS=brc
LK=tlink
```

Change the debug options to

```
CFLAGS=-c -v -mm -WDE -2 -Fm -D_DEBUG -DDLL_VER -D_WINDLL
    -DLIBNAME="$(LIBNAME)" -I$(INCDIR) -DNONAMELESSUNION
LFLAGS=/Twd /c /C /v /Lf:\ole21\lib;f:\bc4\lib
UILIBS=ole2.lib storage.lib
```

Change the "retail" options to

```
CFLAGS=-c -mm -WDE -Fm -2 -DOPTIMIZE -DDLL_VER -D_WINDLL
    -DLIBNAME="$(LIBNAME)" -I$(INCDIR) -DNONAMELESSUNION
LFLAGS=/Twd /c /C /Lf:\ole21\lib;f:\bc4\lib
UILIBS=ole2.lib storage.lib
```

Change the definition of O to

```
O=$(OBJ)^\
```

Next, move the "O" definition to just under the DEBUG= statement near the top of the makefile.

Change GOAL to

```
GOAL: $(O)$(LIBNAME).DLL
```

Remove these lines (you must be sure the directories exist before running make):

```
!if [if not exist $(OBJ)\*. md $(OBJ) >nul]
!error Object subdirectory $(OBJ)\ could not be created
!endif
```

```
!if [if not exist $(OBJ)\NOPC\*. md $(OBJ)\NOPC > nul]
!error non-precompiled header object subdirectory $(OBJ)\NOPC\
   could not be created
!endif


!if [if not exist $(OBJ)\*. md $(OBJ) >nul]
!error Object subdirectory $(OBJ)\ could not be created
!endif


!if [if not exist $(OBJ)\NOPC\*. md $(OBJ)\NOPC > nul]
!error non-precompiled header object subdirectory $(OBJ)\NOPC\
   could not be created
!endif
```

Set these inference rules (replacing the existing ones):

```
{}.c{$(O)}.obj:
        $(CC) -n$(OBJ) @&&!
        $(CFLAGS)  $(@B).c
!


{}.c{$(O)NOPC\}.obj:
        $(CC) -n$(OBJ)\NOPC @&&!
        $(CFLAGS)  $(@B).c!


# compile CPP file into object directory
{}.cpp{$(O)}.obj:
        $(CC) -n$(OBJ) @&&!
        $(CFLAGS) $(@B).cpp
!
```

```
# compile CPP file without precompiled headers into
# object directory\NOPC
# don't compile cpp files etc for localized builds.
{}.cpp{$(O)NOPC\}.obj:
        $(CC) -n$(OBJ)\NOPC @&&!
        $(CFLAGS) $(@B).cpp

!



{}.rc{$(O)}.res:
        $(RS) -I .;$(STDINCDIR);$(RESOURCE)\$(LANG);
          $(RESOURCE)\static -FO $(OBJ)\$(@B).res
          -R $(RFLAGS) $(@B).rc
        if exist $(LIBNAME).dll del $(LIBNAME).dll
```

Remove the INITINSTANCE token from following line:

```
LIBRARY         $(LIBNAME) INITINSTANCE
```

so that it reads

```
LIBRARY         $(LIBNAME)
```

Change the step that begins "$(LK) @<<" to

```
$(LK) $(LFLAGS) @&&!
COD$(MODEL).OBJ $(PRECOMPOBJ) $(DLLOBJS)
$(LIBOBJS),$(O)$(LIBNAME).dll,,$(UILIBS) CRTLDLL.LIB
IMPORT.LIB,$(LIBNAME).def
!
```

Change the following rule and its steps:

```
$(LIBNAME).dll: $(O)$(LIBNAME).dll ole2ui.def
        copy $(O)$(LIBNAME).dll $(LIBNAME).dll
        mapsym -n -l $(LIBNAME).map
        implib -NOWEP $(LIBNAME).lib $(LIBNAME).dll
```

to

```
$(LIBNAME).lib: $(O)$(LIBNAME).dll ole2ui.def
        copy $(O)$(LIBNAME).dll $(LIBNAME).dll
        implib -i $(LIBNAME).lib $(LIBNAME).dll
```

Use this MAKE command line with Borland MAKE:

```
make -N -r -f makedll
```

Good Luck!

The changes in this appendix make it possible for all the programs in this book to compile and run with Borland C. They should work for you, but you should test your code completely to make sure there are no problems introduced by compiling your programs or OLE2UI with a non-Microsoft compiler.

Annotated Bibliography

Brochschmidt, Kraig. *Inside OLE 2*. Redmond, WA: Microsoft Press, 1993.

This book covers OLE in a very detailed way from a C++ perspective. If you want to progress to more advanced topics (such as in-place activation or custom object handlers), you might try this book. Given its size, you can expect to spend more time with it than you did with this book.

DiLascia, Paul. "Ole Made Almost Easy: Creating Containers and Servers Using MFC 2.5," *Microsoft Systems Journal* (April 1994).

This article includes examples of containers and objects that use the Microsoft Foundation Classes (MFC) and C++. It also covers using MFC to support automation.

Microsoft Corporation. *Microsoft Developer's Network CD*,
    Redmond, WA. (Updated quarterly.)

*This CD contains a wealth of information about Windows in general
and OLE in particular. The price may seem a bit steep, but it is well
worth it. You will find the WX server, which uses a VxD to
communicate from DOS to Windows here. You can also find WX
with many Microsoft developer's products (such as the OLE SDK).
There are also numerous articles on DDE and OLE.*

Schulman, Andrew. "Accessing the Windows API from the
    DOS Box," *PC Magazine* (August 1992 and September
    1992).

*Schulman uses the clipboard to pass API calls to a Windows server
in this two part article.*

Shaw, Richard Hale. "Save Multiple Items to the Clipboard
    with CLIPSTAC," *PC Magazine* (August 1992).

*This article shows a technique for saving the clipboard on a stack.
You might adapt this technique to save the clipboard before using the
CLIPSH routines in this book.*

Williams, Al. *Commando Windows Programming*. Reading, MA:
    Addison-Wesley, 1993.

*Many of the simplified Windows programs in this book draw from
techniques you'll find in* Commando Windows Programming.
*You'll also find more about C++ class libraries and a complete
explanation of WPRINT and the PHONE application (before it
became an OLE server).*

Williams, Al. *DOS and Windows Protected Mode*. Reading, MA:
    Addison-Wesley, 1993.

*This book covers protected mode programming under DOS and
Windows. It contains a method for communicating between DOS
and Windows programs that does not rely on the clipboard.*

Glossary

advise An asynchronous notification of an event.

advise sink An OLE object that receives *advises*.

aspect An OLE object's aspect determines how OLE presents its data. For example, OLE can show most objects by their content or with an iconic aspect.

callback A function that Windows calls to notify you of some event. A window procedure is an example of a callback. DDE programs have a special DDE callback to handle DDE events.

class factory An object that creates new objects of a certain class.

client   A program that consumes data from a *server*. A client may consume OLE and DDE data at the same time. Some programs are both clients and servers.

CLSID   A unique identifier for an object class.

Component Object Model   A fundamental part of OLE 2.0, the Component Object Model provides many of the basic services that the object services use.

compound document   An OLE document that contains *embedded* or *linked* objects.

connection   When a DDE *client* requests a *conversation* with a *server*, it connects with the server.

container   Another term for OLE *client*. A container holds objects from an OLE *server*.

conversation   A connection between a DDE client and server. The conversation specifies a *server* and a *topic*. The client may request data on any number of *items* within that topic with a single conversation.

DDEML   The DDE Management Library. This Windows library simplifies the creation of DDE *clients* and *servers*.

delegate   A technique where one object calls another object to perform some function on behalf of a caller. The caller is usually unaware of the delegation.

drag and drop   An OLE 2.0 feature that allows you to transfer data by dragging an object from one OLE application to another. This is similar in form to a clipboard transfer, but the clipboard is not involved. An OLE application can also use drag and drop to move and copy objects internally.

embed   When an OLE *container* contains an embedded object, the container is responsible for storing the object's data and assumes ownership of the object. The container does not need to understand the data; it simply provides a place for the data. Contrast with *link, OLE*.

enumerator   An object that provides functions that return items from another object in some sequence. For example, a format enumerator provides a function that returns valid clipboard formats. Each time a program calls the enumerator, it returns the next value.

inheritance   The ability of one object to inherit methods (functions) from other objects.

interprocess communications   See *IPC*.

IPC   Interprocess Communications. Any method of transferring data between different processes. A process is (loosely) a running program.

item   In a DDE link, the item specifies the particular data of interest. See also: *service name*, and *topic*.

link, cold   A DDE link where the client obtains data from the server one time. If the data subsequently changes, the client will not be aware of the change.

link, DDE   A connection between a DDE *client* and *server* for the purpose of obtaining a single value from the *server*.

link, hot   A DDE link where the *client* automatically receives changed data.

link, OLE   When an OLE *container* has an object that belongs to another document, the object is linked. This takes up very little storage in the container's file and allows multiple containers to share an object economically. When the original application updates the object, all copies will change. Contrast with *embed*.

link, warm   A DDE link where the client receives a notification when the source data changes. The client must still request the data item's new value.

LRPC   Lightweight Remote Procedure Calls. The underlying IPC mechanism behind the current implementation of OLE 2.0. LRPC is lightweight because it will not cross a network. Future versions of OLE may support networking.

marshaling   The process of moving data across process boundaries.

metafile   A file that contains Windows GDI calls. These files store images in a device-independent way.

MFC   Microsoft Foundation Classes. Microsoft's C++ class library that simplifies Windows and OLE programming.

miniserver   An OLE *server* that does not save or load files. These servers must always run in conjunction with an OLE *client*.

moniker   A handle that specifies a data location. Monikers consist of a file path name, and may also specify more detailed locations within a file. For example, a moniker might hold a path reference to a document along with a bookmark name.

notification   A message sent to a program to notify it of some event.

object application   An OLE *server*. An object application provides objects for OLE *containers*.

object handler   A DLL that stands in for an OLE *server* for many operations that an OLE *client* may request. This speeds up operations since the handler executes in the same process space as the *client*. If the handler cannot fulfill the request, it will start the server and *delegate* the request to it.

OLE interface   A set of functions that an OLE object provides to other programs.

OWL   Object Windows Library. A C++ class library by Borland that simplifies Windows programming.

palette   A data structure that determines what colors an image uses.

paste special   A standard OLE dialog that allows you to select the clipboard format for a paste operation.

poke   A method that allows a DDE client to send unsolicited data to a server.

protocol   An older term for *interface*.

REGEDIT   The program you use to edit the *registration database*.

registration database   A systemwide database that Windows maintains for the use of all applications. The database stores information about OLE servers. It also stores data not related to OLE (for example, file associations).

registration key   A key into the *registration database*.

RTF   Rich Text Format. This is a file format that can store text and formatting information such as fonts, graphics, and margins.

SDK   Software Development Kit.

server   A data provider. A DDE server provides data to DDE *clients* and an OLE server works with OLE *clients*. Some applications are both DDE and OLE servers. Also, some programs are both servers and clients.

service name   The name that *clients* use to access a data provider. A DDE server's service name is usually (but not always) the same as its executable name. Clients can learn an OLE server's service name from the *registration database*. A server may supply more than one service by using multiple service names.

storage   A set of *streams* and sub-storages similar to a directory used by the OLE *structured storage system*.

stream   A collection of bytes similar to a file in the OLE *structured storage system*.

string handle   A handle used by DDE programs to share strings between processes.

structured storage system   OLE 2.0 provides this virtual file system that has many advanced features such as long file names and transaction processing. Under MSDOS, the structured storage system can place many *storages* and *streams* in a single MSDOS file.

topic   A DDE server supports topics as part of a three-part data address. A typical server maintains a topic for each open document. See also: *service name* and *item*.

transaction   A DDE transaction consists of a client request and a server response. Transactions may be synchronous (the client does not regain control until the server responds) or asynchronous (the client continues execution immediately).

transaction processing   A file processing methodology that allows you to enter updates to a file and later accept (commit) them or discard (rollback) them.

UUIDGEN   A program used to generate unique *CLSIDs* based on a network card's hardware address.

verb   An action you can perform on an OLE object. Common verbs are Open, Edit, and Play.

VTBL   Table of function pointers that make up an OLE *interface*.

VxD   Virtual Device Driver. These Windows device drivers often do not control a device, but perform advanced system services, such as communicating with DOS programs.

Index

WINBATCH

Special Offer